SOFT DAY

*To my mother —
on her birthday,
26 June 1980.
With Love —
Richard*

SOFT DAY

A Miscellany
of Contemporary Irish Writing

EDITED BY

Peter Fallon & Seán Golden

UNIVERSITY OF NOTRE DAME PRESS

NOTRE DAME   LONDON

Copyright © 1980 by
University of Notre Dame Press
Notre Dame, Indiana 46556

Library of Congress Cataloging in Publication Data

Main entry under title:

Soft day.

1. English literature—Irish authors. 2. English
literature—20th century. I. Fallon, Peter, 1951–
II. Golden, Sean, 1948–
PR8844.S6 1979   820'.8'00914   78-63298
ISBN 0-268-01694-1
ISBN 0-268-01695-X pbk.

Manufactured in the United States of America

Contents

Editors' Notes

THIS BOOK WAS MADE one Summer in Loughcrew. The months that followed allowed small changes and updating. My partnership with Seán Golden evolved naturally from years of my editing and publishing Gallery Books in Ireland and his teaching Irish Studies in American universities and we aimed at presenting a comprehensive survey of contemporary Irish writing.

We had three conditions in mind as we were making our selection: that the author be Irish, alive, and writing in English. We have tried to show the range and scope of our subject by representing authors of various ages —the oldest is 82, the youngest 24—and from every province and social background. At first we thought that we would be able to include only poems and short stories and prose extracts but we have added translations and dramatic pieces. We have featured much new and unfamiliar work and, in almost every case, worked directly with the authors on our choices.

We have included more poetry than any other genre. The comparative brevity of most poems lends to this. Perhaps anyway a single sustained prose or dramatic piece conveys a more satisfying sense of a writer's manner or concerns than a single poem. This book is the first of a series of miscellanies and it is appropriate that poetry be favoured in it because there has been, in the last two decades, phenomenal activity, energy and achievement in this field and the state of poetry in Ireland today is more readily examined and assessed than that of any other form of writing.

Patrick Kavanagh and Austin Clarke succeeded in asserting themselves as major poets after Yeats, and their deaths, in 1967 and 1974 respectively, left a curious gap, a gap that was filled only by the 'election' of comparatively young men, Thomas Kinsella and John Montague, as 'elders' of a continuing resurgence. (Neither John Hewitt nor Richard Murphy lent themselves by character or the nature of their work to this position.) Now the achievements of a whole generation are beginning to crystallise: soon Pearse Hutchinson, Richard Murphy, Thomas Kinsella, James Simmons, Desmond O'Grady, Brendan Kennelly, and Derek Mahon will all have published books of their selected poems. The presence of poetry publishing houses, notably The Dolmen Press, and magazines doubtlessly helped towards this definition.

There were few outlets for prose writers before the institution by David Marcus in 1968 of a weekly *New Irish Writing* page in the Irish Press and the establishment afterwards, from his devotion to the short story, of the Poolbeg Press. The Irish Writers' Co-operative has since been formed to publish short novels and collections of short stories. Apart from Samuel Beckett, the established prose writers worked exclusively in the traditional mode. There are few innovations or experiments—nor need there be—in the stories of Liam O'Flaherty, Sean O'Faolain and Mary Lavin. Now one can discern two strains of composition: one from these writers, through Edna O'Brien, James Plunkett and John McGahern, to younger writers; another from Joyce's later work and Samuel Beckett, through Aidan Higgins, to John Banville, Dermot Healy and Neil Jordan. One suspects the work of younger prose writers might predominate a subsequent miscellany.

Until recently little of the work of living playwrights was being published or maintained in print in Ireland. Our question was whether we should include one complete play or excerpts from a few. We thought the latter course more representative. A number of playwrights might have been included—the work of Brian Friel, Hugh Leonard and Heno Magee is well known or hard to excerpt; others have written perhaps one outstanding play—John B. Keane's *The Field,* for instance, is a work of true dramatic intensity and effect, but his other work lacks the same strength and, possibly, attention—and we chose from three others. Eugene McCabe examines the tensions and personalities of the rural Ireland of his border county; Thomas Murphy's success lies in his examination and treatment of youth, and exile, and the character of small provincial Irish towns; Thomas Kilroy's *Talbot's Box* is more concerned with psychological states, and his triumph lies in his eloquent and lucid interpretation of them. The aim of younger playwrights—Jim and Peter Sheridan, for example—is exclusively for theatrical effect and their plays read less well than one would hope or anticipate.

Remembering Pound's dictum that a country's literature should be translated afresh every generation since the meaning of language changes so rapidly, it is fitting that a version from the Irish by his friend and disciple, Desmond O'Grady, be featured with Eilís Dillon's translation of Eibhlín Dhubh Ní Chonaill's magnificently moving lament. We have included also the last poem in English by Michael Hartnett who now writes in Irish. But this is merely a suggestion of the work being done. A volume of versions in English of the work of modern writers in Irish is presently underway.

Several authors included in this book have been published by the Gallery Press. I like to think that one could not compile a miscellany like this without including many of them and I know that my involvement in *Soft Day* is an extension of the work and ideals of the Gallery Press.

Peter Fallon
The Garden Lodge, 1978.

IRELAND, AN ISLAND smaller than Indiana with a capital no larger than Buffalo, continues its astonishing role as a mainstay in modern literature. Oscar Wilde and George Bernard Shaw enriched the English dramatic tradition. Douglas Hyde, William Butler Yeats, John Millington Synge, Lady Gregory, James Stephens, and George Fitzmaurice reinvigorated Irish literature by voicing traditional, specifically Irish, content in an English identifiably Irish in form, tone, and rhythm. Their work evolved with, then fueled, the revolutionary political movement of their time which culminated, in Ireland, in this century's first war of national liberation, a model for the many that followed. Irish art's political and cultural alienation from received tradition dovetailed with the Modernist revolution developing in European art. James Joyce, in exile, and Sean O'Casey, soon to follow suit, trained their attention on contemporary Dublin, turned their backs on specifically English traditions, and forged new tools and techniques for Irish writers, as did the later Yeats. A period of isolated and insular reconstruction followed the ferment which informed the works of these Masters. This produced masters of its own: Liam O'Flaherty, Frank O'Connor, Sean O'Faolain, Elizabeth Bowen. These writers and their works are well known. They are generally taken to be the standard of Irish writing, their period to be the great moment of modern Irish literary history. But the mid-century produced masters too.

A second generation of modern writers, adapting themselves to new political and socioeconomic conditions on both sides of a border that split Ireland, broke new ground by re-investigating traditions, conventions, and subjects. Austin Clarke, Patrick Kavanagh, Flann O'Brien/Myles na Gopaleen, and Louis MacNeice faced a bewildering array of alternative literary modes: English, Anglo-Irish, Irish (Gaelic), Abbey Theatre and "Irish Revival" conventions, American, the incomparable examples of Yeats, Joyce, Synge, and O'Casey. They accomplished major work in new ways, expanding still further the range of Irish writing. At tragic cost, Brendan Behan's career maintained public consciousness of Irish writers: the myth of the hard-drinking Irish writer expired painfully with

himself and O'Brien and Kavanagh. Only now does this mid-century generation receive the kind of attention showered on the stars of the Revival,
but they are steadily becoming better known, and their work is available.

This book presents a third generation. Contemporary Irish writers face
the same array of traditions and modes as their forebears, as well as the
accumulating examples of their forebears, and the added attractions of international alternatives. When Joyce exiled himself in Europe because
neither Ireland nor England offered him creative sustenance, forging his
own way, he set an example many Irish writers followed. Samuel Beckett,
the best known of these, is Ireland's greatest contemporary writer.
Thomas MacGreevy, Denis Devlin, Brian Coffey, and others of Beckett's
generation, shared the attempt to find new ways of writing in these cosmopolitan circumstances. As the creative centre of writing in English
shifted from England to America and Ireland in this century, a larger
world opened up for Irish writers. Today's writers, inheriting this world,
are producing work which will, in time, rank favourably with their pred-
ecessors', but contemporary Irish writing is not well-known outside of
Ireland, partly because so much attention is focussed upon the events and
works of the first quarter of the century, and so little upon the great
changes occurring as Ireland evolves through the inevitably difficult period of postcolonial adjustment which underlies all aspects of modern
Irish culture.

This selection is quite deliberately a miscellany rather than an anthol-
ogy. It does not attempt to establish canons of taste or to collect the "best
of" the work produced by contemporary Irish writers. Instead it samples
what is currently being written in Ireland, or by Irish writers, providing a
cross section to be updated regularly, a showcase for work as it is produced rather than a museum showcase. Our major difficulty in assembling this selection has been an abundance of suitable material. Ireland
has a wealth of good writers but a dearth of outlets abroad for their work.
Every aspect of contemporary Irish writing is displayed here. Liam O'Flaherty, who spans the revolutionary and contemporary periods, provides
a traditional touchstone. Francis Stuart, a major influence on younger
writers who has now achieved some fame, has been a force in Irish writing for decades. Beckett's work has international stature. John Hewitt has
roots in the Protestant culture of the North of Ireland, and explores relations between the Protestant and Catholic communities there, a topic of
vital concern in Ireland. Mary Lavin, recognized for her mastery of traditional form, depicts parochial life in the South of Ireland. Eilís Dillon's
translation of *Caoineadh Airt Uí Laoghaire* revitalizes that passionate
elegy. Translation itself demonstrates the role literature in Irish still plays
for Irish writers whose primary language is English. Writing in Irish forms

a major component of twentieth century Irish writing, but is unfortunately not represented here because the Irish language is not generally
current among potential readers. Future volumes will contain bilingual
selections of current writing in Irish.

Writers born since Irish independence grew up in an Ireland apprecia-
bly different from that their parents lived in. Their work reflects both
continuities and contrasts in Irish life, and their perceptions of them.
Aidan Higgins approaches fiction from a cosmopolitan vantage point,
while John McGahern examines the claustrophobia of rural Irish life, and
John Jordan the mores of Dubliners. Poets born in the '20s and '30s range
across many personal, political, historical, mythological, philological,
and literary concerns. Their work also demonstrates their acquaintance
with the several traditions of versification in English—Irish, Anglo-Irish,
English, and American—and they range further afield to other languages
and literatures, bringing to their poetry a complex sensitivity to medium
as well as to traditions and subject matter. Pearse Hutchinson is particu-
larly sensitive to minority ethnic groups. Richard Murphy, celebrated for
his long narrative poems, now cultivates a more traditional lyric mode.
Thomas Kinsella transmutes Irish myth, history, and sociology into a
hard, existential vision. John Montague infuses his poetry with both an
intimate knowledge of Irish culture and history and an international
awareness of form and structure. James Simmons, a modern troubadour,
illustrates how northern Irish poets maintain closer ties to contemporary
English poetry than their southern counterparts do. Desmond O'Grady
treats personal concerns from a Modernist perspective on a cycladic
island.

Writers raised in Ireland after World War II show still further devel-
opments in Irish consciousness. For them Ireland's divided political
allegiances often reflect divided cultural allegiances which, in current circumstances, are undergoing profound changes. Writers from both communities in the North often share more in common with each other than
with writers from the South, who differ considerably among themselves
in background, yet remain distinct from northern writers though many
contradictions blur these distinctions. For northern writers English poetry
has remained a dominant influence; for southern writers Irish and American poetry rival English verse. The northern poets presented here repre-
sent both communities. Subject matter and attitudes toward it may differ,
but both groups are evolving an esthetic-in-common and the political and
esthetic ferment evident in their work is very much in-progress. Southern
poets presented here come from different regions, some urban, some
rural, and show a variety of styles and concerns. One of them, Michael
Hartnett, has committed himself to writing poetry in Irish. While poetry

in Ireland generally tends overmuch toward the lyric mode, Derek Mahon and Seamus Heaney have begun turning the wellmade poem convention of current English writing on its ear with their Irish intonations and ironies, and Thomas Kinsella and John Ennis are writing longer, complexly structured poems. The traditional Irish short story form endeared to Frank O'Connor is also still widely, and often too facilely, practiced, too automatically praised, but younger prose writers show signs of breaking out of this recognizably "Irish" mold. Dermot Healy, Neil Jordan, and John Banville write innovative, unselfconsciously Irish fiction, and seem to presage new freedom and life for that form.

In coming years the Irish writers gathered here will gain more recognition. This miscellany is a first step in circulating their work and furthering that aim.

Seán Golden
Ballaghaderreen, 1978

Acknowledgements

FOR PERMISSION TO include the material in this book acknowledgement is made to the following:

John Banville for his extract;
John Calder and the author for Samuel Beckett's adaptation;
Allen Figgis, Victor Gollancz Ltd. and the author for Eavan Boland's poems;
The Irish Press and the author for Edward Brazil's story;
The Blackstaff Press, Wake Forest University Press and the author for Ciaran Carson's poems;
The Gallery Press, Wake Forest University Press and the author for Eiléan Ní Chuilleanáin's poems;
The Gallery Press and the author for Harry Clifton's poems;
The Dolmen Press and the author for Seamus Deane's poems;
The Irish University Review and the author for Eilís Dillon's translation;
The Gallery Press and the author for Paul Durcan's poems;
The Gallery Press and the author for John Ennis's poems;
The Dolmen Press, The Gallery Press, The Deerfield Press and the author for Michael Hartnett's poems;
Dermot Healy for his story;
The Deerfield Press, The Gallery Press and Seamus Heaney for his poems;
The Blackstaff Press, MacGibbon and Kee and the author for John Hewitt's poems;
Aidan Higgins for his extract;
The Gallery Press and the author for Pearse Hutchinson's poems;
The Poolbeg Press and the author for John Jordan's story;
Neil Jordan for his extract;
The Gallery Press and the author for Brendan Kennelly's poems;
The Gallery Press and Thomas Kilroy for his extract;
The Dolmen Press, Peppercanister and the author for Thomas Kinsella's poems;

Mary Lavin for her story;

Victor Gollancz Ltd. and the author for Michael Longley's poems;

The Gallery Press and the author for Eugene McCabe's extract;

Faber and Faber Ltd. and the author for John McGahern's story;

Derek Mahon for his poems;

The Dolmen Press, Wake Forest University Press and the author for John Montague's poems;

Paul Muldoon for his poems;

The Irish University Review and the author for Richard Murphy's poems;

The Gallery Press, The Proscenium Press and the author for Thomas Murphy's extracts;

The Wolfhound Press and the author for Liam O'Flaherty's story;

The Gallery Press and the author for Desmond O'Grady's poems and translation;

Frank Ormsby for his poems;

The Blackstaff Press, The Bodley Head and the author for James Simmons's poems;

The Irish Press and the author for Francis Stuart's story.

SOFT DAY

LIAM O'FLAHERTY

The Mermaid

IN THE VILLAGE of Liscarra there lived a young man who was famous for his strength and beauty. From end to end of the coast his name was like sweet honey on the lips of the people. To strength and comeliness, the two most-coveted virtues in our Western land, Nature had added countless others no less desirable. So that it seemed a young god had come to live among us. Instead of jealousy, it was a godly pride that he aroused in others, young and old; pride that such a one had been born of their race.

In spring-time, when young horses were being broken on the long strand by the seashore, it was Michael McNamara who was chosen to tame the wildest, and no man ever saw him thrown. It was a great joy to hear him shout the wild calls of the horseman as he raced by the sea's edge, with one hand grasping the mane, the other swinging the long halter about his golden head, while the sunlight glittered on the horse's naked hide and the unshod hooves splashed through the foaming wash of the waves. He could throw an ox single-handed with one twist of the beast's horns. People vied with one another to have him in the prow of their boat at sea; both for his skill as an oarsman and because it seemed to them that the cruel sea would not dare to drown one who was the favourite of God.

At church on Sundays young women blushed at their prayers, feeling him in the same house with them.

Most wonderful of all his gifts was the subtle genius of his hands. He could make a boat with wood and a house with stone and a basket with willow rods. Indeed, he seemed to be master of all crafts by the grace of Nature, so that music, which is a special gift among us, mostly always reserved for the blind and the weak as compensation, was also his, in its fullest sweetness. No blackbird at sunset ever sang with finer melody than he, and with a fiddle his fingers wove those wild sweet tunes that have been handed down through many generations from our ancient poets, who, by their divine witchcraft, so it's said, learned the piping of the birds.

Everything prospered with him, yet he coveted nothing, neither wealth

1

nor position; neither did he put his talents to the base purpose of gain, as is customary with the avaricious, but he did everything free, for the love of his neighbours. He lived simply like others less gifted and less fortunate, tilling his land and fishing in the sea and carousing with the young men at festival times.

He was twenty-six when his mother died. She had no other children, and his father had died three months after Michael was born. Such was the young man's innocence that he never shed a tear on his mother's death, and he followed her to her grave smiling. He did not understand the meaning of sorrow. When his relatives rebuked him for his levity, he told them that it would be foolish to mourn for one who had gone to share eternal happiness with the saints.

After his mother's death he lived alone in his house for two years without thought of marriage, although the finest women in the district were offered to his relatives, as is the custom. When the parish priest rebuked him for his celibacy, saying it would lead him into debauchery and sin, he said that a man who had to be muzzled by a wife as a protection against debauchery was not worthy of the joy of innocence. After that people began to treat him with priestly respect.

Then at the great horse fair of Ballintubber, there was a man of the family of Conroy, who had come down from the mountains with three horses for sale. They were three beauties; bred from the same mother, and people remarked that a great sorrow or a greater want must have forced their owner to put himself in the way of parting with them. For among Western people a beautiful horse has no price. McNamara got into conversation with this man, while the jobbers were examining the animals and shouting out their faults to the rage of their owner, who knew them to be without blemish.

'This is a terrible day,' he said, 'for my father's son, to be selling my last three horses to strangers of foul mouths and I that can remember the day when there was a score of horses of that breed grazing free on the mountain. But I have a daughter that has to be portioned.'

'Well!' said McNamara. 'If your daughter is as beautiful as your horses I'll take her without any portion.'

'And who may you be?' said Conroy.

'I am Michael McNamara of Liscarra. I am well-known among my people.'

With that, the stranger shook McNamara by the hand and they retired with their relatives to a tavern, where they drank one another's health, and that evening they all set out to the mountains to see the young woman. When McNamara saw her his innocence and his happiness left him, for she was more beautiful than he.

He took her by the hand, and he said to her:

'It's a poor boast for the young men of your country to say that they let your father drive his horses to the fair to portion you, for you are more beautiful than the morning sun. But you are as cruel as the March wind. I brought your father's horses back from the fair of Ballintubber to his door unsold, and you have numbed my heart in return for this kindness. Now you'll have to marry me, before you add to your cruelty by killing me with desire for you.'

Indeed, desire came upon him with the frenzy of a wild hurricane that comes rushing on a summer day out of the ocean in the west, laying waste all before it. And she was worthy of such love.

When the foam bubbles are flying in the wind above the cliff-tops on an April day and the gay sun, shining through the rain, is mirrored in their watery globes, they are more beautiful than rare pearls. Such were this girl's eyes, jewels of maddening beauty. Her raven hair was haloed by the shimmering light that the full moon casts upon the sea, within dark bays, where rock birds nod upon their ledge, hushed by the enchantment of the night. She was dressed simply, as was fitting for one so beautiful; for the richest clothes would but defile her body, that was made to be adored in its white innocence by wondering eyes, naked, like the pretty flowers that open wide their petals to the bee.

But, alas! Rank weeds that sprout in March still flourish in their ugliness when the autumn winds are singing of the winter's snow, while the most tender blossoms lose their fragrance from dawn to sunset of one summer day. So with this girl. Her beauty was too perfect to endure. Already the red flush of death was on her cheeks.

She returned his love, and on the feast of Saint Martin that autumn Margaret Conroy became the wife of Michael McNamara in the parish church of Liscarra. People shed tears in the church, and a crowd like an army followed them home to the wedding.

They lived together in an ecstasy of happiness for a month. During the rare moments when they were not in one another's arms, McNamara went about like one entranced, overpowered by the amazing passion that had come to him. And she, giving herself with the frenzy of the doomed, burned in the heat of his caresses until, to his horror, one morning he awoke beside her to find the pallor of death on her lips.

She was dead within a week. Wise old women that followed her corpse to the grave said that a convent was the proper place for such frail beauty; that it could only live wedded to the gentle Christ. Others, who still believed in the ancient sorceries, said that the God Crom had taken her for his bride.

McNamara lost his reason. He refused to believe that she was dead and walked behind the coffin in a stupor, but when he saw them lower the coffin into the grave and shovel earth upon it, he uttered a wild shriek and threw himself into the pit. They dragged him out and took him away, still shrieking, but he broke from their arms and ran wild into the country, tearing his hair, wailing aloud, cursing God, his mother and the day he was born. He gashed his face with thorns and tore off his clothes. At last they caught him and brought him home. The people came to comfort him.

When the first outburst of his sorrow had exhausted itself and his reason returned, he said to the people who had come to comfort him:

'Why do ye talk to me about the love of God, who is so cunning in His cruelty? Did I not see her put down into the earth among the worms? Why do ye tell me that time will cure the sorrow of my heart, when I know that from now to my last breath I can only have a curse for the sun that rises with the dawn and for the birds that sing with the fall of night? Go away from me all of you and leave me here alone in this house where I can still feel the sweetness of her breath.'

He who had been as beautiful and meek and happy as a god in his innocence was now uncouth in his sorrow. The people fled from his scowling face. He sat all day by his empty hearth, in silence with his grief. At dead of night, when the terrible moon came shining through the windows of his house, he softened into tears and went barefooted to the bed where he had lain with her. He kissed the pillow which her head had touched, whispering her name. Then she appeared near to him and he forgot the grave in which they had buried her. So he slept. But next morning, when he awoke and found an empty place where she had lain beside him, his anguish returned with greater force. He passed the day, sitting in silence by his cold hearth.

Towards evening the first storm of winter gathered in the east and the thunder of the sea reached the village loudly. Then he heard her calling him. He went out of the house and saw the sea birds in the sky, going inland from the sea that was rising. The sky was magnificent with purple and black clouds and the roar of thunder and the brilliant lightning flashes incited him to a frenzy of delirium, for he thought this tumult was the voice of God, repenting for having stolen his beloved.

He went from the village to the seashore. There, in a rockbound cove, on a sandy place, the village boats were lain. He took one of them, with oars, and pushed it into the tide. And he rowed out to sea. Soon the frail craft was tossing on great breakers and carried westwards by the wind, beneath the towering cliffs.

Then he heard her voice, above the roaring of the wind, singing to him, and he cried out:

'Margaret, my loved one, where are you? I am coming.'

Then his sorrow vanished and his heart grew light and his eyes shone in ecstasy and he rowed towards the cliffs, carried by the great waves, that rolled like mountains to the concave walls of stone. Now he heard her voice clearly, singing to him, quite near, a song of enchanting sweetness. He dropped his oars, stood up in the boat, and turned towards the cliff, whence her voice had come to him.

As the wave carried his boat at headlong speed towards the cliff, he saw her, with her arms stretched out, beckoning to him. Her raven hair was crowned with glittering sea-foam and it streamed down her naked white shoulders. She wore a belt of sea-gems. Her feet were winged. She stood at the door of a cave that had opened in the cliff's face, and beyond her, within the cave, he saw a palace of dazzling beauty.

Then the wave struck the cliff, sending a column of hissing brine high into the firmament, and at the same instant his arms closed about her wraith and he swooned into an ecstasy of eternal love.

FRANCIS STUART

Jacob

An Episode from a Theme Based upon the Biblical Story of Jacob, Laban and His Two Daughters

A WORD ABOUT JACOB MACGREGOR'S background and present circumstances. It's enough, without delving into personal history, to record that this man with the blanched face evidently in the grip of an intense obsession is a widower with a son at school (his third in the course of the year) and a training establishment at the Curragh to which he moved some years previously from the larger family one.

At the break-up of the household there had been grief and bitterness, pain and resentment. No need to go into that. There are traces both of Semite and gypsy blood in him which make it hard to take such things easily. (A Jewish grandfather put the Celtic prefix before the family name of Gregor when he came to Ireland to train horses.)

Jacob took with him to his new quarters the head lad, Corcoran; and, to deepen the rift between himself and his twin brother, the stable jockey, Matt Macey, came and offered him first call on his services the day after the move.

Those are old patterns, faded and bleached in the glare of the pressing present moments in the story. On this latest of which he had come to town and was staying at the hotel owned by a patron of his, Manzini, and had gone out to eat at a restaurant in the same ownership.

Two things were on his mind, both urgent and, as usual, confusing in their apparently opposite compulsions. One was the lift-girl who'd taken him up to his room at his arrival an hour ago, and the other was the thought of his favourite dish that he had come here to order. While awaiting being served he sat with his face that felt too big and exposed at moments of crisis, half covered by one of his hands.

He was shading his eyes, shutting out the rest of the room and trying to have another look at her. Dark. Fragile build. Plain, gold ear-rings. None of this was to the point. Long legs in jeans, simple, white blouse. Equally irrelevant.

What was it that had so disturbed and excited him? (Why were they taking all evening over his order?); the faint luminosity on her brow, grave, lucid, a reflection of the torch of God (his vocabulary, though restricted, was capable of poetry).

At last the *Porchetta veritabile Romana* which he could only get in this restaurant (though his housekeeper Katie Muldoon could make a fair attempt at it when in the mood) was placed before him.

With the flies buzzing round the small table, he ate and ate, filling his mouth with crackling morsels of suckling-pig roasted to a deep bronze and flavoured with garlic and something that he imagined as mandrake (or mandragora root), and washing them down with gulps of the raw Frascati wine.

He felt better, less agitated, more relaxed. That, of course, was a manner of speaking, a short-cut through complex emotions. It did not mean that he wasn't still under the spell of the lift-girl. Her effect on him had been spiritual and sensual at the same time. That was always the trouble with Jacob; he was susceptible to all kinds of conflicting urges. He had an impulse to kneel before her, touch his big mouth to the end of her blue jeans and, on the other hand, if he let himself go, he could imagine, when alone in the lift with her, trying to slip his hand down the front of her blouse.

Soon the heat, the flies (not that it was a cheap joint, far from it), the letters from his son, Joseph, burning in an inside pocket, the Italian wine (at twelve shillings the litre), were combining to produce in him a nervous state of anxious expectation. Manzini (he dropped in for an hour or two each evening to keep an eye on things) came to the table to welcome Jacob whom he'd missed when he arrived at the hotel. Before Manzini could ask about the two-year-old he was training for him, Jacob got in first with his question.

"What girl, Mr. MacGregor?"

He leant towards Jacob, his sallow face thrust right across the small table, waiting to be told about the colt and not really having heard what he'd been asked.

"The elevator-operator."

"That's my daughter, Mr. MacGregor. A very shy girl."

"I thought I noticed a resemblance," Jacob lied to explain his curiosity.

"You did? Nobody ever said that before. She's a difficult kid, Mr. MacGregor. She keeps her sign permanently at 'stop', never lets it change to 'wait' or 'go'. Not like my other girl behind the reception desk."

Two daughters, both working in the hotel; but Jacob wasn't to be deflected by the father's rather blatant mention of the second. With Manzini there was always a degree of crudity. This also applied to his questions about Johnny. Jacob had to try to indicate to him some of the subtleties and uncertainties involved in running a two-year-old in only his second race.

"There are colts (I've seldom known it to happen with fillies) who slumber the best part of their first season away. That's how its been with our fellow, he wasn't fully awake in his only race. It wasn't until the last couple of furlongs that he began to get the hang of what was going on. Matt Macey could tell the exact moment he woke up under him."

Manzini was hanging on every word, bewildered, suspicious and hopeful.

"You reckon he is wide awake now?"

"That's something I'll be able to tell when I saddle him in his box tomorrow."

"You must have some idea as to how he'll run, that's all I'm asking."

Manzini was breathing right across the table, his black eyes on Jacob as if to try to detect what he thought was willfully being withheld from him.

Next morning Jacob was up early, reckoning, correctly, that it was his best chance of being alone in the lift with Miss Manzini. He had noted her slight limp and used it as an excuse to start a more intimate conversation than one on the weather.

"I'm not a doctor but I know something about muscular trouble."

"It's not muscular."

Did she think it strange how often he went to his room and came down again in the course of the morning? But she didn't as much as smile when the door slid open and there he was again. They were not always alone, and it was during the fifth or sixth ascent and descent before he got her to tell him that she suffered from the effects of a car crash a year or so before in which her mother had been killed.

There was no one waiting for the elevator in the hall on that occasion and, still talking, she pressed the button that closed the door and took him up with her again.

After her physical injuries had healed she was left with an intermittent humming or buzzing in her head. She only heard it lying down and, at first, she had thought the sound came from under the pillow.

They had told her at the hospital that the noises were caused by a nervous condition which would clear up in the course of time, but they were becoming more insistent.

Later that morning when Jacob was driving Manzini to the course the latter announced:

"I'm afraid it's bad news, Mr. MacGregor."

Jacob, with thoughts now on the coming race, had supposed that whatever news there was (he'd been talking to his head lad, Corcoran, on the phone) would come from him.

"I mean about my little girl. I should have told you last night, she's more or less of an invalid, suffers from some nervous trouble. But my elder daughter, you haven't met her yet, she's another story altogether. I'll introduce you to her this evening."

"Oh, I was only . . . "

Manzini interrupted: "Don't let it bother you. When we get back to town tonight you can take Lucy out, she's a little *Nectarino,* and you won't give another thought to Pietà. That's a promise, Mr. MacGregor."

This sort of talk embarrassed Jacob. The last words struck him as especially crude, as if he was being offered the elder girl as some sort of incentive or reward.

The rain that had been falling all morning increased as they drove towards the course. Jacob was keeping an eye out for a break in the clouds. The softer the ground the greater the test for the little colt whom he hadn't yet managed to put the work into that would have left him hard and fit. But when the stands and racecourse buildings loomed up it was in a wet glimmer against a dark curtain of rain.

He dropped Manzini at the entrance to the course and, after parking the car, went to the stables. Corcoran was sitting on a pile of straw in a corner of Johnny's box, his back to the wall, with a folded sheet of newspaper on his drawn-up knees which he was pretending to read in the dim light coming in over the open top half of the door. He made a move to get up, but Jacob told him to stay where he was.

"How's everything?"

"Middling, Mr. MacGregor."

Corcoran's eyes under the low brim of the hat he wore in all weather, indoors and out, were neither on his master nor the sheet of newspaper but had never left a spot on the flat of the colt's neck.

Jacob knew he liked to preserve an atmosphere of melancholy before a race on which much depended, seeming to believe that, being lived through beforehand, the way was left clearer for a happy outcome.

The rain gurgling in a down pipe from a gutter over the stable door increased the sense of anxiety.

Jacob ran a hand along Johnny's flank and the skin flowed along under his palm and then slipped back in its own strong counter-current. The horse was beginning to sense that something was going to be asked of him that hadn't been before.

Drip . . . gurgle . . . drip. A clatter of hooves on brick, a rattle of buckets and, from the distance, the first eerie notes as the bookies from under their wide umbrellas started calling the odds on the first race. Johnny raised his bony head with the pale star aglimmer at the top of the narrow front, and Corcoran gave a murmur.

"What's that?" Jacob asked anxiously.

"Just telling him there's nothing to worry about. You're not going to ad-vise his owner to back him, Mr. MacGregor?"

"I don't know yet."

"There's a couple of animals in the race whose connections don't care what happens to them as long as they land the money today."

Corcoran had been talking to the other travelling lads.

Jacob didn't go to look for Manzini when he got to the course. He moved around with an idea that he might hear or notice something that would give him some idea of the strength of the opposition in the two-year-old event. Though he knew that this was a vain hope. Those trainers with likely runners in the same race seemed to avoid him, with a perfunctory: "Afternoon, MacGregor," or a passing: "How-are-you, Jamie" (he was called James or Jamie by most of his colleagues). Though by now he was so tense that he might be imagining all this.

He took a look at the horses parading for the first race and then at the bookmakers' boards which, however, didn't yet concern him. He was drawn several times to the far end of the grand stand to peer out in the di-rection from which the clouds were coming.

He saw to it that he didn't meet Manzini until shortly before the race in which Johnny was running when he was waiting in the centre of the pa-rade ring which on these occasions has something about it of a church cer-emonial, a wedding or a procession in honour of a saint, with the jockeys decked out in their silks, the burnished colts and fillies placing their hooves with pious delicacy on the gravelly aisle as they're led round.

But this bit of formal pageantry always made Jacob doubly aware of the foam-flecked, sweaty consummation in which all was going to end. He suffered from pre-race nerves to a degree that nobody would have guessed from what he thought of as his coarse-grained exterior.

Matt Macey came up in Manzini's brown and silver hoops, brown sleeves, and touched his cap with the perfunctory gesture of a jockey who knows that from now on all is in his hands.

"Keep him up handy with the leaders if I can, sir, and smack him one if I have to when it comes to it?" Macey asked from out of the side of his mouth away from the colt's owner.

"Right. Except that you don't touch him with the whip, Matt."

"And if it comes to a tight finish?" Manzini enquired.

The jockey's face remained blank, a yellowish mask the texture of dried appleskin. He took in nothing at these moments except the few words Jacob spoke in a certain low tone that got through the shutter he'd pulled down. What Manzini or anybody else said didn't touch him. He stood be-tween trainer and owner, bow-legged in his white breeches, arms akimbo, head on one side (a bright-plumaged bird about to take off) quite motion-less but for a twitch of the whip that sprouted from under his left elbow.

After Jacob had given him a leg up he went with Manzini to the rails where the bookmakers stood.

Hey, what was this? Manzini was thrusting a bundle of notes, five- and ten-pound ones, into his hands.

"Put these on with your own."

This wasn't the right sort of sign at all. What Jacob had been hoping for was the recollection of some small incident, not fully grasped at the time, from the training grounds, that he could suddenly interpret in a way that would clear up the uncertainty.

"No, you haven't given me much encouragement, Mr. MacGregor. But I know it's not your way. I heard what you told the jockey and that's enough."

Jacob took the notes and put them into his pocket. Then, in a low tone, he made their combined bet on credit with a bookie whom he knew. Immediately all along the line of blackboards the odds against Johnny's name were rubbed out. Without waiting to see what price was being substituted he followed Manzini onto the part of the stand marked: "Owners and trainers only."

Races, for those deeply involved, tend to divide into three acts, each of about twenty seconds (if it's a five-furlong affair) on the electric clock. (A timing that has no correspondence to the duration as measured on the inner chronometer.)

In the first of these phases covering, say, two furlongs, and still far-removed even through binoculars, there's a feeling of relief, even of lei-sureliness, after the tension of the preliminaries. So it was now. For those fleeting seconds Jacob could have been a distant spectator of some colour-ful and unhurried display on a summer afternoon. Except that he still had had, right up to the "off", one eye on the clouds. Though another shower couldn't make any difference to the going, this sudden darkening of the scene added to the feeling that all judgement based on knowledge of the colt's capabilities and a study of the form of the other runners was having its last frail validity washed away out there behind the rain-mist.

Then came the second phase when names are strung out by the race commentator like the words of a litany, some repeated, some soon dis-carded, while through the curtain of rain and a momentary gap in the on-coming wall, he saw the silver and brown hoops, silver cap.

"Holy Mother, where is he?"

Only Manzini muttering in his sleep. Of which no notice need be taken. Phase three began as soon as Jacob could make out Macey nestled down on Johnny in the middle of the field, no doubt catching through hands and knees the intimations coming from the colt, and with the corners of his eyes registering signs and portents from the runners nearest him.

"Mamma mia, is he going to get beaten?"

"Just a moment, Manzini."

This was the vital test when Matt Macey was conveying to his mount that, far from it being time to relax his pull on the bit and take a breather, that the moment of moments had come (as it hadn't in his only other race) to drop the head lower and extend the swing of forelegs a few extra inches.

Now, too, was the moment when, for the participating spectator, the last yards before the winning post seem to have a lurid green spot-light trained on them as the protagonists appear in the final agonising scene before the curtain falls.

"He didn't get up, eh? How was it? The jockey left it too bloody late, didn't he?"

Manzini's muttering was the buzzing of a wasp close to Jacob's blanched, damp face.

"Was he beaten? That's what I'm asking you, Mr. MacGregor."

"It's a photograph. We've got to sit and suffer a bit longer."

Leave it still in doubt. Keep it quiet as long as possible. Hoard up the treasure. Say nothing apart from a nod exchanged with Corcoran and a low word of congratulation to Macey, as he took off the saddle in the winner's enclosure.

SAMUEL BECKETT

(an English adaptation from the French of Robert Pinget)

The Old Tune

Background of street noises. In the foreground a barrel-organ playing an old tune. 20 seconds. The mechanism jams. Thumps on the box to set it off again. No result.

GORMAN *(old man's cracked voice, frequent pauses for breath even in the middle of a word, speech indistinct for want of front teeth, whistling sibilants).* There we go, bust again. *(Sound of lid raised. Scraping inside box.)* Cursed bloody music! *(Scraping. Creaking of handle. Thumps on box. The mechanism starts off again.)* Ah about time!

Tune resumes. 10 seconds. Sound of faltering steps approaching.

CREAM *(old man's cracked voice, stumbling speech, pauses in the middle of sentences, whistling sibilants due to ill-fitting denture).* —Well, if it isn't—*(the tune stops)*—Gorman my old friend Gorman, do you recognise me Cream father of the judge, Cream you remember Cream.

GORMAN. Mr. Cream! Well, I'll be! Mr. Cream! *(Pause.)* Sit you down, sit you down, here, there. *(Pause.)* Great weather for the time of day Mr. Cream, eh.

CREAM. My old friend Gorman, it's a sight to see you again after all these years, all these years.

GORMAN. Yes indeed, Mr. Cream, yes indeed, that's the way it is. *(Pause.)* And you, tell me.

CREAM. I was living with my daughter and she died, then I came here to live with the other.

GORMAN. Miss Miss what?

CREAM. Bertha. You know she got married, yes, Moody the nurseryman, two children.

13

GORMAN. Grand match, Mr. Cream, grand match, more power to you. But tell me then the poor soul she was taken then was she.

CREAM. Malignant, tried everything, lingered three years, that's how it goes, the young pop off and the old hang on.

GORMAN. Ah dear oh dear Mr. Cream, dear oh dear.

Pause.

CREAM. And you your wife?

GORMAN. Still in it, still in it, but for how long.

CREAM. Poor Daisy yes.

GORMAN. Had she children?

CREAM. Three, three children, Johnny, the eldest, then Ronnie, then a baby girl, Queenie, my favourite, Queenie, a baby girl.

GORMAN. Darling name.

CREAM. She's so quick for her years you wouldn't believe it, do you know what she came out with to me the other day ah only the other day poor Daisy.

GORMAN. And your son-in-law?

CREAM. Eh?

GORMAN. Ah dear oh dear, Mr. Cream, dear oh dear. (*Pause.*) Ah yes children that's the way it is. (*Roar of motor engine.*) They'd tear you to flitters with their flaming machines.

CREAM. Shocking crossing, sudden death.

GORMAN. As soon as look at you, tear you to flitters.

CREAM. Ah in our time Gorman this was the outskirts, you remember, peace and quiet.

GORMAN. Do I remember, fields it was, fields, bluebells, over there, on the bank, bluebells. When you think. . . . (*Suddenly complete silence. 10 seconds. The tune resumes, falters, stops. Silence. The street noises resume.*) Ah the horses, the carriages, and the barouches, ah the barouches, all that's the dim distant past, Mr. Cream.

CREAM. And the broughams, remember the broughams, there was style for you, the broughams.

Pause.

GORMAN. The first car I remember well I saw it here, here, on the corner, a Pic-Pic she was.

CREAM. Not a Pic-Pic, Gorman, not a Pic-Pic, a Dee Dyan Button.

GORMAN. A Pic-Pic, a Pic-Pic, don't I remember well, just as I was coming out of Swan's the bookseller's beyond there on the corner, Swan's the bookseller's that was, just as I was coming out with a rise of fourpence ah there wasn't much money in it in those days.

CREAM. A Dee Dyan, a Dee Dyan.

GORMAN. You had to work for your living in those days, it wasn't at six you knocked off, nor at seven neither, eight it was, eight o'clock, yes by God. (*Pause.*) Where was I? (*Pause.*) Ah yes eight o'clock as I was coming out of Swan's there was the crowd gathered and the car wheeling round the bend.

CREAM. A Dee Dyan Gorman, a Dee Dyan, I can remember the man himself from Wougham he was the vintner what's this his name was.

GORMAN. Bush, Seymour Bush.

CREAM. Bush that's the man.

GORMAN. One way or t'other, Mr. Cream, one way or t'other no matter it wasn't the likes of nowadays, their flaming machines they'd tear you to shreds.

CREAM. My dear Gorman do you know what it is I'm going to tell you, all this speed do you know what it is it has the whole place ruinated, no living with it any more, the whole place ruinated, even the weather. (*Roar of engine.*) Ah when you think of the springs in our time remember the springs we had, the heat there was in them, and the summers remember the summers would destroy you with the heat.

GORMAN. Do I remember, there was one year back there seems like yesterday must have been round 95 when we were still out at Cruddy, didn't we water the roof of the house every evening with the rubber jet to have a bit of cool in the night, yes summer 95.

CREAM. That would surprise me Gorman, remember in those days the rubber hose was a great luxury a great luxury, wasn't till after the war the rubber hose.

GORMAN. You may be right.

CREAM. No may be about it, I tell you the first we ever had round here was in Drummond's place, old Da Drummond, that was after the war 1920 maybe, still very exorbitant it was at the time, don't you remember watering out of the can you must with that bit of a garden you had didn't you, wasn't it your father owned that patch out on the Marston Road.

GORMAN. The Sheen Road Mr. Cream but true for you the watering you're right there, me and me hose how are you when we had no running water at the time or had we.

CREAM. The Sheen Road, that's the one out beyond Shackleton's sawpit.

GORMAN. We didn't get it in till 1925 now it comes back to me the wash-hand basin and jug.

Roar of engine.

CREAM. The Sheen Road you saw what they've done to that I was out on it yesterday with the son-in-law, you saw what they've done our little gardens and the grand sloe hedges.

GORMAN. Yes all those gazebos springing up like thistles there's trash for you if you like, collapse if you look at them am I right.

CREAM. Collapse is the word, when you think of the good stone made the cathedrals nothing to come up to it.

GORMAN. And on top of all no foundations, no cellars, no nothing, how are you going to live without cellars I ask you, on piles if you don't mind, piles, like in the lake age, there's progress for you.

CREAM. Ah Gorman you haven't changed a hair, just the same old wag he always was. Getting on for seventy-five is it?

GORMAN. Seventy-three, seventy-three, soon due for the knock.

CREAM. Now Gorman none of that, none of that, and me turning seventy-six, you're a young man Gorman.

GORMAN. Ah Mr. Cream, always the great one for a crack.

CREAM. Here Gorman while we're at it have a fag, here. (*Pause.*) The daughter must have whipped them again, doesn't want me to be smoking, mind her own damn business. (*Pause.*) Ah I have them, here, have one.

GORMAN. I wouldn't leave you short.

CREAM. Short for God's sake, here, have one.

Pause.

GORMAN. They're packed so tight they won't come out.

CREAM. Take hold of the packet. (*Pause.*) Ah what ails me all bloody thumbs. Can you pick it up.

Pause.

GORMAN. Here we are. (*Pause.*) Ah yes a nice puff now and again but it's not what it was their gaspers now not worth a fiddler's, remember in the forces the shag remember the black shag that was tobacco for you.

CREAM. Ah the black shag my dear Gorman the black shag, fit for royalty the black shag fit for royalty. (*Pause.*) Have you a light on you.

GORMAN. Well then I haven't, the wife doesn't like me to be smoking.

Pause.

CREAM. Must have whipped my lighter too the bitch, my old tinder jizzer.

GORMAN. Well no matter I'll keep it and have a draw later on.

CREAM. The bitch sure as a gun she must have whipped it too that's going beyond the beyonds, beyond the beyonds, nothing you can call your own. (*Pause.*) Perhaps we might ask this gentleman. (*Footsteps approach.*) Beg your pardon Sir trouble you for a light.

Footsteps recede.

GORMAN. Ah the young nowadays Mr. Cream very wrapped up they are the young nowadays, no thought for the old. When you think, when you think. . . . (*Suddenly complete silence. 10 seconds. The tune resumes, falters, stops. Silence. The street noises resume.*) Where were we? (*Pause.*) Ah yes the forces, you went in in 1900, 1900, 1902, am I right?

CREAM. 1903, 1903, and you 1906 was it?

GORMAN. 1906 yes at Chatham.

CREAM. The Gunners?

GORMAN. The Foot, the Foot.

CREAM. But the Foot wasn't Chatham don't you remember, there it was the Gunners, you must have been at Caterham, Caterham, the Foot.

GORMAN. Chatham I tell you, isn't it like yesterday, Morrison's pub on the corner.

CREAM. Harrison's, Harrison's Oak Lounge, do you think I don't know Chatham. I used to go there on holiday with Mrs. Cream, I know Chatham backwards Gorman, inside and out, Harrison's Oak Lounge on the corner of what was the name of the street, on a rise it was, it'll come back to me, do you think I don't know Harrison's Oak Lounge there on the corner of dammit I'll forget my own name next and the square it'll come back to me.

GORMAN. Morrison or Harrison we were at Chatham.

CREAM. That would surprise me greatly, the Gunners were Chatham do you not remember that?

GORMAN. I was in the Foot, at Chatham, in the Foot.

CREAM. The Foot, that's right the Foot at Chatham.

GORMAN. That's what I'm telling you, Chatham the Foot.

CREAM. That would surprise me greatly, you must have it mucked up with the war, the mobilisation.

GORMAN. The mobilisation have a heart it's as clear in my mind as yesterday the mobilisation, we were shifted straight away to Chesham, was it, no, Chester, that's the place, Chester, there was Morrison's pub on the corner and a chamber-maid, Mr. Cream, a chamber-maid what was her name, Joan, Jean, Jane, the very start of the war when we still didn't believe it, Chester, ah those are happy memories.

CREAM. Happy memories, happy memories, I wouldn't go so far as that.

GORMAN. I mean the start up, the start up at Chatham, we still didn't believe it, and that chamber-maid what was her name it'll come back to me. (*Pause.*) And your son by the same token.

Roar of engine.

CREAM. Eh?

GORMAN. Your son the judge.

CREAM. He has rheumatism.

GORMAN. Ah rheumatism, rheumatism runs in the blood Mr. Cream.

CREAM. What are you talking about, I never had rheumatism.

GORMAN. When I think of my poor old mother, only sixty and couldn't move a muscle. (*Roar of engine.*) Rheumatism they never found the remedy for it yet, atom rockets is all they care about, I can thank my lucky stars touch wood. (*Pause.*) Your son yes he's in the papers the Carton affair, the way he managed that case he can be a proud man, the wife read it again in this morning's *Lark*.

CREAM. What do you mean the Barton affair.

GORMAN. The Carton affair Mr. Cream, the sex fiend, on the Assizes.

CREAM. That's not him, he's not the Assizes my boy isn't, he's the County Courts, you mean Judge . . . Judge . . . what's this his name was in the Barton affair.

GORMAN. Ah I thought it was him.

CREAM. Certainly not I tell you, the County Courts my boy, not the Assizes, the County Courts.

GORMAN. Oh you know the Courts and the Assizes it was always all six of one to me.

CREAM. Ah but there's a big difference Mr. Gorman, a power of difference, a civil case and a criminal one, quite another how d'you do, what would a civil case be doing in the *Lark* now I ask you.

GORMAN. All that machinery you know I never got the swing of it and now it's all six of one to me.

CREAM. Were you never in the Courts?

GORMAN. I was once all right when my niece got her divorce that was when was it now thirty years ago yes thirty years, I was greatly put about I can tell you the poor little thing divorced after two years of married life, my sister was never the same after it.

CREAM. Divorce is the curse of society you can take it from me, the curse of society, ask my boy if you don't believe me.

GORMAN. Ah there I'm with you the curse of society look at what it leads up to, when you think my niece had a little girl as good as never knew her father.

CREAM. Did she get alimony.

GORMAN. She was put out to board and wasted away to a shadow, that's a nice thing for you.

CREAM. Did the mother get alimony.

GORMAN. Divil the money. (*Pause.*) So that's your son ladling out the divorces.

CREAM. As a judge he must, as a father it goes to his heart.

GORMAN. Has he children.

CREAM. Well in a way he had one, little Herbert, lived to be four months then passed away, how long is it now, how long is it now.

GORMAN. Ah dear oh dear, Mr. Cream, dear oh dear and did they never have another?

Roar of engine.

CREAM. Eh?

GORMAN. Other children.

CREAM. Didn't I tell you, I have my daughters' children, my two daughters. (*Pause.*) Talking of that your man there Barton the sex boyo isn't that nice carryings on for you showing himself off like that without a stitch on him to little children might just as well have been ours Gorman, our own little grandchildren.

Roar of engine.

GORMAN. Mrs. Cream must be a proud woman too to be a grandmother.

CREAM. Mrs. Cream is in her coffin these twenty years Mr. Gorman.

GORMAN. Oh God forgive me what am I talking about, I'm getting you wouldn't know what I'd be talking about, that's right you were saying you were with Miss Daisy.

CREAM. With my daughter Bertha, Mr. Gorman, my daughter Bertha, Mrs. Rupert Moody.

GORMAN. Your daughter Bertha that's right so she married Moody, gallous garage they have there near the slaughter-house.

CREAM. Not him, his brother the nursery-man.

GORMAN. Grand match, more power to you, have they children?

Roar of engine.

CREAM. Eh?

GORMAN. Children.

CREAM. Two dotey little boys, little Johnny I mean Hubert and the other, the other.

GORMAN. But tell me your daughter poor soul she was taken then was she. (*Pause.*) That cigarette while we're at it might try this gentleman. (*Footsteps approach.*) Beg your pardon Sir trouble you for a light. (*Footsteps recede.*) Ah the young are very wrapped up Mr. Cream.

CREAM. Little Hubert and the other, the other, what's this his name is. (*Pause.*) And Mrs. Gorman.

GORMAN. Still in it.

CREAM. Ah you're the lucky jim Gorman, you're the lucky jim, Mrs. Gorman by gad, fine figure of a woman Mrs. Gorman, fine handsome woman.

GORMAN. Handsome, all right, but you know, age. We have our health thanks be to God touch wood. (*Pause.*) You know what it is Mr. Cream, that'd be the way to pop off chatting away like this of a sunny morning.

CREAM. None of that now Gorman, who's talking of popping off with the health you have as strong as an ox and a comfortable wife, ah I'd give ten years of mine to have her back do you hear me, living with strangers isn't the same.

GORMAN. Miss Bertha's so sweet and good you're on the pig's back for God's sake, on the pig's back.

CREAM. It's not the same you can take it from me, can't call your soul your own, look at the cigarettes, the lighter.

GORMAN. Miss Bertha so sweet and good.

CREAM. Sweet and good, all right, but dammit if she doesn't take me for a doddering old drivelling dotard. (*Pause.*) What did I do with those cigarettes?

GORMAN. And tell me your poor dear daughter-in-law what am I saying your daughter-in-law.

CREAM. My daughter-in-law, my daughter-in-law, what about my daughter-in-law.

GORMAN. She had private means, it was said she had private means.

CREAM. Private means ah they were the queer private means, all swallied up in the war every ha'penny do you hear me, all in the bank the private means not as much land as you'd tether a goat. (*Pause.*) Land Gorman there's no security like land but that woman you might as well have been talking to the bedpost, a mule she was that woman was.

GORMAN. Ah well it's only human nature, you can't always pierce into the future.

CREAM. Now now Gorman don't be telling me, land wouldn't you live all your life off a bit of land damn it now wouldn't you any fool knows that unless they take the fantasy to go and build on the moon the way they say, ah that's all fantasy Gorman you can take it from me all fantasy and delusion, they'll smart for it one of these days by God they will.

GORMAN. You don't believe in the moon what they're experimenting at.

CREAM. My dear Gorman the moon is the moon and cheese is cheese what do they take us for, didn't it always exist the moon wasn't it always there as large as life and what did it ever mean only fantasy and delusion Gorman, fantasy and delusion. (*Pause.*) Or is it our forefathers were a lot of old bags maybe now is that on the cards I ask you, Bacon, Wellington, Washington, for them the moon was always in their opinion damn it I ask you you'd think to hear them talk no one ever bothered his arse with the moon before, make a cat swallow his whiskers they think they've discovered the moon as if as if. (*Pause.*) What was I driving at?

Roar of engine.

GORMAN. So you're against progress are you.

CREAM. Progress, progress, progress is all very fine and grand, there's such a thing I grant you, but it's scientific, progress, scientific, the moon's not progress, lunacy, lunacy.

GORMAN. Ah there I'm with you progress is scientific and the moon, the moon, that's the way it is.

CREAM. The wisdom of the ancients that's the trouble they don't give a rap or a snap for it any more, and the world going to rack and ruin, wouldn't it be better now to go back to the old maxims and not be gallivanting off killing one another in China over the moon, ah when I think of my poor father.

GORMAN. Your father that reminds me I knew your father well. (*Roar of engine.*) There was a man for you old Mr. Cream, what he had to say he lashed out with it straight from the shoulder and no humming and hawing, now it comes back to me one year there on the town council my father told me must have been wait now till I see 95, 95 or 6, a short while before he resigned, 95 that's it the year of the great frost.

CREAM. Ah I beg your pardon, the great frost was 93 I'd just turned ten, 93 Gorman the great frost.

Roar of engine.

GORMAN. My father used to tell the story how Mr. Cream went hell for leather for the mayor who was he in those days, must have been Overend yes Overend.

CREAM. Ah there you're mistaken my dear Gorman, my father went on the council with Overend in 97, January 97.

GORMAN. That may be, that may be, but it must have been 95 or 6 just the same seeing as how my father went off in 96, April 96, there was a set against him and he had to give in his resignation.

CREAM. Well then your father was off when it happened, all I know is mine went on with Overend in 97 the year Marrable was burnt out.

GORMAN. Ah Marrable it wasn't five hundred yards from the door five hundred yards Mr. Cream, I can still hear my poor mother saying to us ah poor dear Maria she was saying to me again only last night, January 96 that's right.

CREAM. 97 I tell you, 97, the year my father was voted on.

GORMAN. That may be but just the same the clout he gave Overend that's right now I have it.

CREAM. The clout was Oscar Bliss the butcher in Pollox Street.

GORMAN. The butcher in Pollox Street, there's a memory from the dim distant past for you, didn't he have a daughter do you remember.

CREAM. Helen, Helen Bliss, pretty girl, she'd be my age, 83 saw the light of day.

GORMAN. And Rosie Plumpton bonny Rosie staring up at the lid these thirty years she must be now and Molly Berry and Eva what was her name Eva Hart that's right Eva Hart didn't she marry a Crumplin.

CREAM. Her brother, her brother Alfred married Gertie Crumplin great one for the lads she was you remember, Gertie great one for the lads.

GORMAN. Do I remember, Gertie Crumplin great bit of skirt by God, hee hee hee great bit of skirt.

CREAM. You old dog you!

Roar of engine.

GORMAN. And Nelly Crowther there's one came to a nasty end.

CREAM. Simon's daughter that's right, the parents were greatly to blame you can take it from me.

GORMAN. They reared her well then just the same bled themselves white for her so they did, poor Mary used to tell us all we were very close in those days lived on the same landing you know, poor Mary yes she used to say what a drain it was having the child boarding out at Saint Theresa's can you imagine, very classy, daughters of the gentry Mr. Cream, even taught French they were the young ladies.

CREAM. Isn't that what I'm telling you, reared her like a princess of the blood they did, French now I ask you, French.

GORMAN. Would you blame them Mr. Cream, the best of parents, you can't deny it, education.

CREAM. French, French, isn't that what I'm saying.

Roar of engine.

GORMAN. They denied themselves everything, take the bits out of their mouths they would for their Nelly.

CREAM. Don't be telling me they had her on a string all the same the said young lady, remember that Holy Week 1912 was it or 13.

Roar of engine.

GORMAN. Eh?

CREAM. When you think of Simon the man he was don't be telling me that. (*Pause.*) Holy Week 1913 now it all comes back to me is that like as if they had her on a string what she did then.

GORMAN. Peace to her ashes Mr. Cream.

CREAM. Principles, Gorman, principles without principles I ask you. (*Roar of engine.*) Wasn't there an army man in it.

GORMAN. Eh?

CREAM. Wasn't there an army man in it.

GORMAN. In the car?

CREAM. Eh?

GORMAN. An army man in the car?

CREAM. In the Crowther blow-up.

Roar of engine.

GORMAN. You mean the Lootnant St. John Fitzball.

CREAM. St. John Fitzball that's the man, wasn't he mixed up in it?

GORMAN. They were keeping company all right. (*Pause.*) He died in 14. Wounds.

CREAM. And his aunt Miss Hester.

GORMAN. Dead then these how many years is it now how many.

CREAM. She was a great old one, a little on the high and mighty side perhaps you might say.

GORMAN. Take fire like gunpowder but a heart of gold if you only knew. (*Roar of engine.*) Her niece has a chip of the old block wouldn't you say.

CREAM. Her niece? No recollection.

GORMAN. No recollection, Miss Victoria, come on now, she was to have married an American and she's in the Turrets yet.

CREAM. I thought they'd sold.

GORMAN. Sell the Turrets is it they'll never sell, the family seat three centuries and maybe more, three centuries Mr. Cream.

CREAM. You might be their historiographer Gorman to hear you talk, what you don't know about those people.

GORMAN. Histryographer no Mr. Cream I wouldn't go so far as that but Miss Victoria right enough I know her through and through we stop and have a gas like when her aunt was still in it, ah yes nothing hoity-toity about Miss Victoria you can take my word she has a great chip of the old block.

CREAM. Hadn't she a brother.

GORMAN. The Lootnant yes, died in 14. Wounds.

Deafening roar of engine.

CREAM. The bloody cars such a thing as a quiet chat I ask you. (*Pause.*) Well I'll be slipping along I'm holding you back from your work.

GORMAN. Slipping along what would you want slipping along and we only after meeting for once in a blue moon.

CREAM. Well then just a minute and smoke a quick one. (*Pause.*) What did I do with those cigarettes? (*Pause.*) You fire ahead don't mind me.

GORMAN. When you think, when you think. . . .

Suddenly complete silence. 10 seconds. Resume and submerge tune a moment. Street noises and tune together crescendo. Tune finally rises above them triumphant.

JOHN HEWITT

O Country People

O country people, you of the hill farms,
huddled so in darkness I cannot tell
whether the light across the glen is a star,
or the bright lamp spilling over the sill,
I would be neighbourly, would come to terms
with your existence, but you are so far;
there is a wide bog between us, a high wall.

I've tried to learn the smaller parts of speech
in your slow language, but my thoughts need more
flexible shapes to move in, if I am to reach
into the hearth's red heart across the half-door.

You are coarse to my senses, to my washed skin;
I shall maybe learn to wear dung on my heel,
but the slow assurance, the unconscious discipline
informing your vocabulary of skill,
is beyond my mastery, who have followed a trade
three generations now, at counter and desk;
hand me a rake, and I at once, betrayed,
will shed more sweat than is needed for the task.

If I could gear my mind to the year's round,
take season into season without a break,
instead of feeling my heart bound and rebound
because of the full moon or the first snowflake,
I should have gained something. Your secret is pace.
Already in your company I can keep step,
but alone, involved in a headlong race,
I never know the moment when to stop.

I know the level you accept me on,
like a strange bird observed about the house,
or sometimes seen out flying on the moss

that may tomorrow, or next week, be gone,
liable to return without warning
on a May afternoon and away in the morning.

But we are no part of your world, your way,
as a field or a tree is, or a spring well.
We are not held to you by the mesh of kin;
we must always take a step back to begin,
and there are many things you never tell
because we would not know the things you say.

I recognize the limits I can stretch;
even a lifetime among you should leave me strange,
for I could not change enough, and you will not change;
there'd still be levels neither'd ever reach.

And so I cannot ever hope to become,
for all my goodwill toward you, yours to me,
even a phrase or a story which will come
pat to the tongue, part of the tapestry
of apt response, at the appropriate time,
like a wise saw, a joke, an ancient rime
used when the last stack's topped at the day's end,
or when the last lint's carted round the bend.

The Scar

There's not a chance now that I might recover
one syllable of what that sick man said,
tapping upon my great-grandmother's shutter,
and begging, I was told, a piece of bread,
for on his tainted breath there hung infection
rank from the cabins of the stricken west,
the spores from black potato-stalks, the spittle
mottled with poison in his rattling chest;
and she, who, by her nature, quickly answered,
accepted in return the famine-fever;
and that chance meeting, that brief confrontation,
conscribed me of the Irishry for ever.

Though much I cherish is outside their vision,
and much they prize I have no claim to share,
yet in that woman's death I found my nation:
the old wound aches and shows its fellow-scar.

An Irishman in Coventry

A full year since, I took this eager city,
the tolerance that laced its blatant roar,
its famous steeples and its web of girders,
as image of the state hope argued for,
and scarcely flung a bitter thought behind me
on all that flaws the glory and the grace
which ribbon through the sick, guilt-clotted legend
of my creed-haunted, Godforsaken race.
My rhetoric swung round from steel's high promise
to the precision of the well-gauged tool,
tracing the logic in the vast glass headlands,
the clockwork horse, the comprehensive school.

Then, sudden, by occasion's chance concerted,
in enclave of my nation, but apart,
the jigging dances and the lilting fiddle
stirred the old rage and pity in my heart.
The faces and the voices blurring round me,
the strong hands long familiar with the spade,
the whiskey-tinctured breath, the pious buttons,
called up a people endlessly betrayed
by our own weakness, by the wrongs we suffered
in that long twilight over bog and glen,
by force, by famine and by glittering fables
which gave us martyrs when we needed men,
by faith which had no charity to offer,
by poisoned memory, and by ready wit,
with poverty corroded into malice,
to hit and run and howl when it is hit.

This is our fate: eight hundred years' disaster,
crazily tangled as the Book of Kells:

the dream's distortion and the land's division,
the midnight raiders and the prison cells.
Yet like Lir's children banished to the waters
our hearts still listen for the landward bells.

The Sheep Skull

As we came up the steep familiar lane,
famous for berries, brimmed with meadowsweet,
and bright with rose-hips in season, every rut
was stiff with frost and rigid as a bone;
and in the dead red bracken at one side
a sheep skull lay exposed, as though the year
had yielded all, had nothing more to hide,
and shaped this symbol to make all things clear.

We stopped. You poked your stick into the hole
the spine had entered, raised the sculpture up:
my left hand took it in a steady grip,
my right drew off a horn with easy pull;
then, with more labour, we dislodged its twin
and dropped the bare mask back into the grass.
One horn for powder dry when foes draw in,
and one to toast each danger as we pass.

MARY LAVIN

A Voice from the Dead
A Monologue

THE MISSES CONIFFE, NOT being married, were unsparing of their services to the Ladies Altar Society of Castlerampart, the town of their birth. It was they who undertook the laundering of altar linens, communion cloths and surplices, the polishing of the brass candelabra and altar vases, as well as the disposal of withered flowers, ferns and pot plants. They also undertook the recruitment of fresh flowers from all gardens in the town other than their own, which understandably produced few blooms. However, in consequence of this dedication, Miss Theresa and her sister Sara had come to enjoy a privilege previously accorded only to old Luke Humphries, the sacristan—the privilege of staying behind in the chapel after evening devotions when the rest of the congregation had been herded out into the chapel yard by old Luke and the votive candles quenched. Then, the chapel door firmly bolted, Miss Theresa withdrew to the sacristy, there to attend to the numerous tasks awaiting her, medals to be sewn to Confirmation rosettes, candle-grease to be removed from the various articles, rents to be repaired in sodality banners. Sara Coniffe remained in the body of the chapel to tiptoe about with old Luke, peering under kneelers and pews in search of any mortuary cards, rosary beads or other pious items let fall by the pious in the fervour of prayer. Such items if found were, by tradition, placed on the ledge of the nearest window, where they lay until such time as they were espied, identified and repossessed by their owners.

Except for the occasional grating noise of a pew being straightened, a respectful silence was observed by all. However, one evening in early Spring, a second after the doors were bolted, there was a loud and sudden rapping on a side-aisle door, and a peremptory voice called out for admittance.

"A Voice from the Dead" by Mary Lavin is one of a series of short stories taken and re-written by the author from her early novel *The House in Clewe Street*. She believes that this work plus her novel *Mary O'Grady* should have been composed as collections of short stories from the start.

"Let me in, Luke Humphries! Let me in! Do you hear me? It's me, Mrs. Mulloy." To the elder Miss Coniffe, in the sacristy, the voice was sufficiently indistinct to be ignored. Moreover, assuming that old Luke, too, would turn a deaf ear to the unseemly clamour, she went on with her stitching. But in the darkening body of the church Mrs. Mulloy's every word was heard, and heard with the compulsive force of a voice from the pulpit. "Listen to me, Luke Humphries. I've lost my cousin Lottie's mortuary card. It must have fallen out of my prayer book. Let me in at once. I want to look for it."

Sara, who happened to be standing just under the sanctuary lamp, in the pool of its red light, could only marvel that Mrs. Mulloy had detected so quickly the loss of one mortuary card among the hundreds that swelled her prayer book to the size of another woman's handbag.

"I'll look for it, Luke?" she whispered. "When I find it, you can hand it out to her?" But Luke, having feigned deafness to the clamour of Mrs. Mulloy, could hardly betray that he had heard Miss Sara's timid whisper. Instead he stomped over to a confessional box and began to open and close the doors, for no good reason that Sara could see.

The voice came again.

"The poor soul would turn in her grave if she thought I'd left my only memento of her lying all night on the window-ledge of a cold, empty church!"

"Oh, Luke," Sara wailed so piteously Luke stomped back and opened up the great oak door.

Next minute Mrs. Mulloy was sailing down the centre aisle towards the pew she habitually occupied, and standing up on the seat, she groped along the window ledge. "Don't tell me it's not there," she cried, in stricken tones, which however, gave way to loud thanksgivings as, grovelling on her hands and knees, she recovered her lost property—a mortuary card lavishly edged with paper lace, and so monumental in size it had had to be folded in two to fit into a prayer book. "I would not have wished for all the world to lose it," she said, addressing herself to Sara, who, unlike Luke, had lacked the presence of mind to vanish, "because of a solemn promise I made to Lottie." Then, as a draught caused the sanctuary light to sway and its ruby rays to tremble, Mrs. Mulloy lowered her voice, though it was not certain whether this was in deference to the Perpetual Presence or in awe of her own promise to the dead. She held up the card. "The strange thing is that I missed it before I got as far as the chapel gates. And I want to tell you, Sara, there is very little doubt in my mind that, this night, I have been in the presence of a force beyond my poor earthly power to fathom." Here, without further preamble, she launched into her story. "I was just about to leave the chapel yard, Sara, and go

about my business as I've done all my life, when I noticed that the gates—
and for that matter the chapel railings as well—were shockingly in need
of a coat of paint. Now, considering it must be seven years since they
were painted, isn't it a strange thing it was on this night of all others I noticed the condition of those gates? And from noticing it, I naturally went
on to thinking it our duty as parishioners to point out to Father Drew
what ought to be done—the person undertaking this duty not, of course,
being myself, seeing as how my daughter is married to a painter. I know
only too well, and so do you, Sara, the odd constructions that can be put
on an innocent word in this town. Indeed some of us might have been better to have had our mouth sewn up, a thing my own mother was always
threatening to get done to me when I was a child—God rest her soul, as
well as that of Lottie." Pausing to cross herself, Mrs. Mulloy here permitted herself a slight digression. "Though mind you, Sara, when it comes to
putting in a word in praise of our own, more can often be lost than gained,
by refraining. If we don't praise them, are there many likely to praise
them for us?" She sadly shook her head. "Few. Very few. Furthermore,
you won't, I trust, mind my saying this, Sara, but if your own mother,
who is dead and gone now with Lottie and the rest—God grant eternal
peace to all their souls—if your mother had not been so behind-hand in
coming forward with a hint, in certain well-chosen quarters, of the for-
tune that you and your sisters would inherit—I mean before it was too
late—there's no knowing but you and Theresa might both be married
now, and your money not useless to everyone—including yourselves.
Not but I've heard whispers, Sara, that there won't be much of that for-
tune left if your sister Lily's husband is let get his hands on it. That, of
course, is no business of mine. And, I will say this, he's a good-looking
man. Your sister Lily was lucky to collar him. Don't we all know it's better for a woman to marry any sort of a man, than no man at all. Are you
listening to me, Sara?"

"You were telling me about your cousin Lottie," Sara said faintly.

"Ah, yes, poor Lottie. The minute I noticed the condition of those
gates—"

"Yes? What happened?" Sara said less faintly, having become aware
that her sister Theresa had closed the sacristy door.

"I am trying to tell you, Sara. I wish you'd stop interrupting me," Mrs.
Mulloy said. "Well, when I saw the rust on those gates, and decided
something should be done about the matter, I got to thinking how bright
and shiny the gates used to be when I was a child. In those days, Sara, the
chapel and the chapel-yard were considered the safest places for children
to play. On wet days we ran about inside the chapel, playing hide and
seek in the confessional boxes and behind the statues. On fine days we

stayed outside in the chapel-yard, jumping over the graves, or chasing an odd rat, with no one to complain about us shrieking and screaming. You realise of course, Sara, that I'm not speaking of the new cemetery? I never approved of that new place being opened so far outside the town. To be honest I never thought people would permit themselves to be put down in it. I have to allow though that it's well populated now. It will soon be as overcrowded as the old place, but at least here the plots are roomy, with plenty of space for all the family. Even distant connections can be fitted in, if they have no place of their own to go. We children knew the name of every living soul under the sod here, because, when we'd get tired of play-ing we used to pull up fistfuls of grass and rub the moss off the headstones to show up the lettering. We kept the place as clean as our own back yards. The older people used to laugh at us—all except Lottie. When Lot-tie passed and saw us cleaning up a grave she used to call me over and whisper to me that if a bird should happen to fall his dirty droppings on her grave-stone—after she was dead—that she hoped I'd wipe off the mess. Poor Lottie, she was always brooding over her final end, certain each moment would be her last. She often brought me into her house to show me the shroud she'd bought a few days after she married Matty— you remember Matty—the Lord have mercy on him too, poor man. From the start Matty took a poor view of her purchase. He hated the sight of that shroud. In fact, Sara, between ourselves, he went on a batter every time she took it out to air it—which she did regularly—say of a fine Spring day like today. She used to throw it over a bush in the garden to take out the creases and make sure that moths would not consume it before its time. Matty couldn't really be blamed for his carry-on, I suppose, seeing he was a good ten years older than Lottie, and seeing they didn't get on too well together from the start. Though, mind you, some people thought he ought to have been glad of a reminder of the day she'd take her depar-ture, which might be sooner than you'd have believed from the look of her, a stout woman with a good, strong colour in her face. But no! Matty took a poor view of her preparations for the next world. And such prepa-rations! The shroud was only the beginning. The next thing she did was get a cardboard box fitted up with all the necessaries for Extreme Unction in case of her call coming when there was no one around who knew the lay-out of the house. She had the oil and the blessed candle, the crucifix, the rosary beads and the bottle of holy water, as well as a square of linen as stiff as a board for under her chin when she'd be getting communion. Not to mention a towel and a bowl for water for the priest to wash his hands when all would be over. She was bent on ordering her coffin too, I believe, and storing it under the stairs, but Matty put his foot down on

the coffin. Although again you'd think he'd welcome the sight of it coming into the house, to put him in mind of the day he'd be shouldering it out
again. But he had a long wait, God help him. Poor Lottie, in spite of her
prophecies, wasn't called to her reward for thirty-seven years, in spite of
having her bag packed, as you might put it. And by that time the very
people who used to be tittering at her in her lifetime had the mortification
of seeing better grave-cloths on the corpse than they had on their own
beds, and better worsted in her shroud than in the clothes on their own
backs. But that was nothing. When they opened her closet what did they
find but a stack of mortuary cards, all printed with her name and her
picture—as nice a picture as she'd ever had taken—when she was a young
girl, standing by a rosebush in her garden at home before she ever laid
eyes on Matty, much less married him. Just look at that. The best of
paper! And where would you get paper lace now, except perhaps on doy-
leys, or Valentines, and *they're* not black. There's no date on it, of course,
but Lottie was never over-anxious to disclose her age. Anyway, I recall
her saying once that such details didn't matter. All that mattered was to
get as many indulgenced prayers as possible on to a card—as many as it
could hold—each prayer carrying nothing less than three hundred days'
indulgence. She never could make any sense—and neither could I—of
people wasting their time saying prayers that earned them only a hundred
days, when there were other prayers the same length that could get them
three hundred. She was always a great one for good value. She had all the
envelopes addressed and stamped ready to be dropped in the post. I suppose she wanted to make sure they'd be sent to those she could rely on for
prayers. The only flaw in the poor creature's plan was that most of those
the envelopes were addressed to were dead long before herself, and those
envelopes had to be thrown in the fire. Matty, I'm glad to say, had the wit
to steam off the stamps, and I was given to understand he sold them for a
nice penny. The rest of us got the shock of our lives when we got our card
in the handwriting of the corpse we'd just seen coffined. I have to tell you,
Sara, there was a bit of commotion in some houses when the postman delivered the cards. One particular person—whose name cannot be re-
vealed because there was talk at the time of a law case being taken against
poor Matty—but this particular person, who was ill at the time, hadn't
been told that Lottie was no more, and this person took such a turn at the
sight of a card in the hand of the corpse, she fell in a faint and hit her head
off the brass bed-head in her own room. She was buried the day after Lottie. Poor Lottie: she didn't get many prayers from that source. But of
course Lottie couldn't have held it against that person like she could have
held it against me, if I failed her. You see, Lottie made me give my solemn

promise never to look at her face on that mortuary card, without saying a prayer for her immortal soul. And I kept that promise faithfully up until yesterday, when the prayer book I've had all my life finally fell apart, and I had to buy a new one. Things not being done nowadays on the same scale as in Lottie's day, my new prayer book is in no way to be compared with my old one. Lottie's card wouldn't fit into it without me folding it in two, as you can see. Unfortunately, and in order to protect her photograph, I folded it so the picture was on the inside, which meant of course that Lottie could not, as you might say, keep her eye on me. If I'd left it sticking out, the edges would have frayed away to nothing, but Lottie would have fared better, and not have been put to such lengths as she was tonight to communicate with me. You are of course aware, Sara, of what I'm driving at? Ever since I bought the new prayer book, poor Lottie must have been trying to get in touch with me. She must have known I'd break my promise, which I did! But Lottie was always a determined woman. It must have been her who saw to it that my prayer book fell on the floor tonight and the contents were strewn about, and all this without me being nudged or jostled by anyone. Then when I picked them all up—as I thought—unbeknownst I left Lottie's card behind. Then when devotions ended and Luke began quenching the candles—although it can't be said I'm the first to jump up when the priest leaves the altar—I have to admit to having a sensitive nose and I can't stand the smell of guttering-out candles, I went out of the chapel and poor Lottie would not have got a prayer out of me from that time until such time as Father Drew takes it into his head to have the church decorated—which won't be for many a day, I'd be bound, him being a bit of a miser, priest or no priest. But lo and behold, when I reached the chapel gates and saw the rust on them, I was put in mind of how spick and span they used to be when I was a child. And from that I was put in mind of how we used to play in the chapelyard. Of course, from that, it was only a hop, a step and a jump to remembering the promise Lottie extracted from me. There and then I stopped dead in my tracks to fold her mortuary card the other way around with the face looking out at me. And then what? Well, I shouldn't have to tell you! But I will. I opened the prayer book and saw at once there was no sign of Lottie's card. That was when I ran back and banged on the door to be let in to look for it. You know the rest! There it was on the floor! Did you ever hear anything stranger than that? Oh, some say the dead are dead. But after tonight I'll never be persuaded that they haven't a way of getting through to us if they are determined on it."

Suddenly Mrs. Mulloy stopped short. "Good Heavens, I still haven't said a prayer for her! Excuse me Sara!" Going down on one knee she speedily dispatched her duty to the dead and scrambled to her feet again. Then, realising the time she'd wasted on the one person in the town who had little or no conversation with which to repay the prodigality of those who had, with a brisk good night, she let herself out into the fresh, night air.

EILÍS DILLON

(translated from the Irish of Eibhlín Dhubh Ní Chonaill)

The Lament for Arthur O'Leary

I

EIBHLÍN DHUBH: My love forever!
The day I first saw you
At the end of the market-house,
My eye observed you,
My heart approved you,
I fled from my father with you,
Far from my home with you.

II

I never repented it:
You whitened a parlour for me,
Painted rooms for me,
Reddened ovens for me,

This lament was composed by Arthur O'Leary's widow, Eibhlín Dhubh (Dark Eileen) immediately after his death in 1773. . . . Part of the poem purports to have been composed by (his) father and by his sister, but Eibhlín Dhubh is of course the author of the whole work.

Its impact at the time may be judged from the fact that it has been preserved orally for almost two hundred years. . . . It is in no sense a folk poem. Eileen O'Connell was probably the last member of the old school of Irish poets. . . . Poetry was a family tradition . . . and there is evidence to show that the family were patrons of poetry. . . . The rhythm, with its fascinating variations which have been followed as closely as possible, seems new in Irish poetry.

. . . [Arthur O'Leary] was a captain in the Austrian army, [and by] wearing his silver-hilted sword in public he was breaking the law, since he was a Catholic. . . . He seems to have enjoyed baiting the local Protestant gentry—four years af-

Baked fine bread for me,
Basted meat for me,
Slaughtered beasts for me;
I slept in ducks' feathers
Till midday milking-time,
Or more if it pleased me.

III

My friend forever!
My mind remembers
That fine spring day
How well your hat suited you,
Bright gold banded,
Sword silver-hilted—
Right hand steady—
Threatening aspect—
Trembling terror
On treacherous enemy—
You poised for a canter
On your slender bay horse.
The Saxons bowed to you,
Down to the ground to you,
Not for love of you
But for deadly fear of you,
Though you lost your life to them,
Oh my soul's darling.

---

ter his marriage to Eileen O'Connell there was a reward of twenty pounds offered
for him by . . . Abraham Morris . . . who later caused his death. The immediate
cause of his murder was that at Macroom races Arthur O'Leary's horse beat Morris's horse in a race and Morris in a fury invoked the old Penal Law that any Protestant could buy the horse of a Catholic, no matter what its value, for five pounds.
Arthur O'Leary refused to sell the horse and had to go on the run. . . .
He amused himself for a while by showing himself to [Morris and some soldiers pur-
suing him] just out of range of their guns. . . . He crossed the river at Carriganima
. . . and stopped there to look back. But he had misjudged the distance and one
of the soldiers shot him dead. . . . His epitaph, said to have been composed also
by his wife, is just discernible . . . in English:

Lo! Arthur Leary, generous, handsome, brave,
Slain in his bloom, lies in this humble grave.
Died May 4th, 1773, Aged 26 years.

from the translator's preface

IV

Oh white-handed rider!
How fine your brooch was
Fastened in cambric,
And your hat with laces.
When you crossed the sea to us,
They would clear the street for you,
And not for love of you
But for deadly hatred.

V

My friend you were forever!
When they will come home to me,
Gentle little Conor
And Farr O'Leary, the baby,
They will question me so quickly,
Where did I leave their father.
I'll answer in my anguish
That I left him in Killnamartyr.
They will call out to their father;
And he won't be there to answer.

VI

My friend and my love!
Of the blood of Lord Antrim,
And of Barry of Allchoill,
How well your sword suited you,
Hat gold-banded,
Boots of fine leather,
Coat of broadcloth,
Spun overseas for you.

VII

My friend you were forever!
I knew nothing of your murder
Till your horse came to the stable
With the reins beneath her trailing,
And your heart's blood on her shoulders
Staining the tooled saddle
Where you used to sit and stand.

My first leap reached the threshold,
My second reached the gateway,
My third leap reached the saddle.

VIII

I struck my hands together
And I made the bay horse gallop
As fast as I was able,
Till I found you dead before me
Beside a little furze-bush.
Without Pope or bishop,
Without priest or cleric
To read the death-psalms for you,
But a spent old woman only
Who spread her cloak to shroud you—
Your heart's blood was still flowing;
I did not stay to wipe it
But filled my hands and drank it.

IX

My love you'll be forever!
Rise up from where you're lying
And we'll be going homewards.
We'll have a bullock slaughtered,
We'll call our friends together,
We'll get the music going.
I'll make a fine bed ready
With sheets of snow-white linen,
And fine embroidered covers
That will bring the sweat out through you
Instead of the cold that's on you!

X

ART'S SISTER: My friend and my treasure!
There's many a handsome woman
From Cork of the sails
To the bridge of Toames
With a great herd of cattle
And gold for her dowry,
That would not have slept soundly
On the night we were waking you.

XI

EIBHLÍN DHUBH: My friend and my lamb;
You must never believe it,
Nor the whisper that reached you,
Nor the venomous stories
That said I was sleeping.
It was not sleep was on me,
But your children were weeping,
And they needed me with them
To bring their sleep to them.

XII

Now judge, my people,
What woman in Ireland
That at every nightfall
Lay down beside him,
That bore his three children,
Would not lose her reason
After Art O'Leary
That's here with me vanquished
Since yesterday morning?

XIII

ART'S FATHER: Bad luck to you, Morris!—
May your heart's blood poison you!
With your squint eyes gaping!
And your knock-knees breaking!—
That murdered my darling,
And no man in Ireland
To fill you with bullets.

XIV

My friend and my heart!
Rise up again now, Art,
Leap up on your horse,
Make straight for Macroom town,
Then to Inchigeela back,
A bottle of wine in your fist,
The same as you drank with your dad.

XV

EIBHLÍN DHUBH: My bitter, long torment
That I was not with you
When the bullet came towards you,
My right side would have taken it
Or a fold of my tunic,
And I would have saved you
Oh smooth-handed rider.

XVI

ART'S SISTER: My sore sharp sorrow
That I was not behind you
When the gun-powder blazed at you,
My right side would have taken it,
Or a fold of my gown,
And you would have gone free then
Oh grey-eyed rider,
Since you were a match for them.

XVII

EIBHLÍN DHUBH: My friend and my treasure!
It's bad treatment for a hero
To lie hooded in a coffin,
The warm-hearted rider
That fished in bright rivers,
That drank in great houses
With white-breasted women.
My thousand sorrows
That I've lost my companion.

XVIII

Bad luck and misfortune
Come down on you, Morris!
That snatched my protector,
My unborn child's father:
Two of them walking
And the third still within me,
And not likely I'll bear it.

XIX

My friend and my pleasure!
When you went out through the gateway
You turned and came back quickly,
You kissed your two children,
You kissed me on the forehead,
You said: 'Eileen, rise up quickly,
Put your affairs in order
With speed and with decision.
I am leaving home now
And there's no telling if I'll return.'
I mocked this way of talking,
He had said it to me so often.

XX

My friend and my dear!
Oh bright-sworded rider,
Rise up this moment,
Put on your fine suit
Of clean, noble cloth,
Put on your black beaver,
Pull on your gauntlets.
Up with your whip;
Outside your mare is waiting.
Take the narrow road east,
Where the trees thin before you,
Where streams narrow before you,
Where men and women will bow before you,
If they keep their old manners—
But I fear they have lost them.

XXI

My love and my treasure!
Not my dead ancestors,
Nor the deaths of my three children,
Nor Domhnall Mór O'Connell,
Nor Connall that drowned at sea,
Nor the twenty-six years woman
Who went across the water
And held kings in conversation—

It's not on all of them I'm calling
But on Art who was slain last night
At the inch of Carriganima!—
The brown mare's rider
That's here with me only—
With no living soul near him
But the dark little women of the mill,
And my thousand sorrows worsened
That their eyes were dry of tears.

XXII

My friend and my lamb!
Arthur O'Leary,
Of Connor, of Keady,
Of Louis O'Leary,
From west in Geeragh
And from east in Caolchnoc,
Where berries grow freely
And gold nuts on branches
And great floods of apples
All in their seasons.
Would it be a wonder
If Ive Leary were blazing
Besides Ballingeary
And Guagán of the saint
For the firm-handed rider
That hunted the stag down,
All out from Grenagh
When slim hounds fell behind?
And Oh clear-sighted rider,
What happened last night?
For I thought to myself
That nothing could kill you
Though I bought your habit.

XXIII

ART'S SISTER: My friend and my love!
Of the country's best blood,
That kept eighteen wet-nurses at work,
And each received her pay—
A heifer and a mare,

A sow and her litter,
A mill at the ford,
Yellow gold and white silver,
Silks and fine velvets,
A holding of land—
To give her milk freely
To the flower of fair manhood.

XXIV

My love and my treasure
And my love, my white dove!
Though I did not come to you,
Nor bring my troops with me,
That was no shame to me
For they were all enclosed
In shut-up rooms,
In narrow coffins,
In sleep without waking.

XXV

Were it not for the small-pox
And the black death
And the spotted fever,
That powerful army
Would be shaking their harness
And making a clatter
On their way to your funeral,
Oh white-breasted Art.

XXVI

My love you were and my joy!
Of the blood of those rough horsemen
That hunted in the valley,
Till you turned them homewards
And brought them to your hall,
Where knives were being sharpened,
Pork laid out for carving
And countless ribs of mutton,
The red-brown oats were flowing
To make the horses gallop—

Slender, powerful horses
And stable-boys to care them
Who would not think of sleeping
Nor of deserting their horses
If their owners stayed a week,
Oh brother of many friends.

XXVII

My friend and my lamb!
A cloudy vision
Came last night to me
In Cork at midnight
Alone in my bed:
That our white court fell,
That the Geeragh withered,
That your slim hounds were still
And the birds without sweetness
When you were found vanquished
On the side of the mountain,
Without priest or cleric
But an old shrivelled woman
That spread her cloak over you,
Arthur O'Leary,
While your blood flowed freely
On the breast of your shirt.

XXVIII

My love and my treasure!
And well they suited you,
Five-ply stockings,
Boots to your knees,
A three-cornered Caroline,
A lively whip,
On a frisky horse—
Many a modest, mannerly maiden
Would turn to gaze after you.

XXIX

EIBHLÍN DHUBH: My love forever!
And when you went in cities,

Strong and powerful,
The wives of the merchants
All bowed down to you
For they knew in their hearts
What a fine man in bed you were,
And what a fine horseman
And father for children.

XXX

Jesus Christ knows
I'll have no cap on my head,
Nor a shift on my back,
Nor shoes on my feet,
Nor goods in my house,
Nor the brown mare's harness
That I won't spend on lawyers;
That I'll cross the seas
And talk to the king,
And if no one listens
That I'll come back
To the black-blooded clown
That took my treasure from me.

XXXI

My love and my darling!
If my cry were heard westwards
To great Dérrynare
And to gold-appled Capling,
Many swift, hearty riders
And white-kerchiefed women
Would be coming here quickly
To weep at your waking,
Beloved Art O'Leary.

XXXII

My heart is warming
To the fine women of the mill
For their goodness in lamenting
The brown mare's rider.

XXXIII

May your black heart fail you,
Oh false John Cooney!
If you wanted a bribe,
You should have asked me.
I'd have given you plenty:
A powerful horse
That would carry you safely
Through the mob
When the hunt is out for you,
Or a fine herd of cattle,
Or ewes to bear lambs for you,
Or the suit of a gentleman
With spurs and top-boots—
Though it's sorry I'd be
To see you done up in them,
For I've always heard
You're a piddling lout.

XXXIV

Oh white-handed rider,
Since you are struck down,
Rise and go after Baldwin,
The ugly wretch
With the spindle shanks,
And take your revenge
For the loss of your mare—
May he never enjoy her.
May his six children wither!
But no bad wish to Máire
Though I have no love for her,
But that my own mother
Gave space in her womb to her
For three long seasons.

XXXV

My love and my dear!
Your stooks are standing,
Your yellow cows milking;

On my heart is such sorrow
That all Munster could not cure it,
Nor the wisdom of the sages.
Till Art O'Leary returns
There will be no end to the grief
That presses down on my heart,
Closed up tight and firm
Like a trunk that is locked
And the key is mislaid.

XXXVI

All you women out there weeping,
Wait a little longer;
We'll drink to Art son of Connor
And the souls of all the dead,
Before he enters the school—
Not learning wisdom or music
But weighed down by earth and stones.

AIDAN HIGGINS

Letters concerning Bornholm,
Knepp at the Third River

HERS THE NAME OF an island, Bornholm out in the Oltic Sea, beyond Nom and Negur, midway between Omlam and Dansk Yab. She wrote, sometimes in longhand, more often typing:

"Sunday evening, the 6th of July 1975., Negahnepoc.

My dearest Arnold—

Negahnepoc is very hot this weeks. Persiko has taken care of Marijke all the week-end, I needed very much to be alone, been bussy with idiotic things the last weeks, everything at home one Big Mess, not a clean plate or clean cloth. I've been (am) in one of my eternal recomming depressions when all is extra difficult to pretent effectively, I'm far-off, far-off, cannot get out of my own figments, the same themes turn and grow and change but are still the same.

Now I am through the outside mess and have used the rest of the week-end to try to make a fair copy of bewildered notes during the week and it became definately bad: a row of highflown inexact words, neither prosa nor poetry, without genuine sensations, a row of odd oldfashioned assertions which do not hit.

I am very depressed.

If I never learn to write proberly I can nothing in this world. I am clever to nothing, nothing at all. It is all approats, attemps, giving up, making dreams, useless dreams, hoping a little again . . . I complaine. I promised myself never to complain to you and especialy not about this matter.

Letters from Anna Bornholm to Professor Arnold Kauffmann, from the novel *Schönberg's Last Pupil.*

49

Now I have done. Now I have been a native woman thrown out of white man's tent because of bad manners.

In a way I remember you so well. Your brightness. Is anything called that? I can't stand to use the dictionary all the time. My only force is to make guess, hope they fit somebody, something. Thinking over things they disappear to me. Intellectual thing at least. They must come as a cut or they vanish as you say. You give me new words, too, I could fall in love in the H'Silgne language. Sometimes I'm going to do. When I am thinking over feelings they don't vanish. Opperset, they crows. Because you don't think feelings, I guess. How can I live my life? Who is paying for dreams? Why do I need food? Why do I need *thing*? (That damned things). Who do I not live on a Keerg island? Why is the world so sluggish a material? Down again: Why can't I make it light?
I am ashame to complain. Will do it again and again. Tell me to shut up.

10/7: You say nothing about I Ching? Nonsense for you? (Old stuff hanging over Anna's head). Persiko always laugh when I absorbed (dictionary) in that kind of matters, but contempt me too, think it is a complicated and childish stage-setting (dictionary) or rather depriving (dictionary) of a obvious reality, understandable for a child of five. Same Persiko got me to laugh so heartily and painfull (in Ksnadish: 'Tgiletrejh go tgiltrems', a thorough-fucked-wordpair) the other day when he said: "When you feel your thoughts collect to complain, beat your head into the wall."
I'm beating my head into the wall now. Again. Oh I miss you. Again. Forgive me my love that I miss you again too much. Just red your mad letter again (Arnold-again-Arnold-again Arnold-Arnold-again), long parts without rest, I think I mean stop, pause, long breath, fading out and starting again, long breath from a love which wants to empty both body and mind. How can you write like that Arnold, how can you do it against us, how can you make me suffering that much? Sometimes I'm catched by a great anger to you, you demand, no you give the feeling of present but still you are not here, you prevent me to live here by keeping me there, I am longing and prevented, I am kept in imaginations and must drown myself in home-made wine and over-excitement, sometimes I'm catched by a great anger to you. Then it disappears and I must laugh of myself.

For Cosima your wife I have blended feelings. I perceive her, actually, as very sympatical, beautiful and intelligent, too, but obviously wrong for you. As me and my Persiko ('Perversiko, as you call him) apart from that we are through the hate. It alarms me that you still quarrel. Then a long way is left before you are mine. You have had your youth together with her, you have together with her on the impossible beds of your youth and have wished—more fervently than ever since in your life—to make love to her. You (Arnold and Cosima) have had the trust together about you as the famous componist and herself as a beautiful woman in company with gifted men who everybody was secret in love with her, I guess. And you have had the child together, your son Alexander. You have had a life together. Yes, I'm jealous, jealous so it hurts in my teeth, my teeth turn soft in my mouth of jealous.

That I must type my envelopes shock me directly. If you told Cosima about me then she must know that I'm writing to you? Shall I put a false name, too? I have the address of Lindermann from a wrong addressed envelope, preserved it because I knew that you are fond of him in a special way. It would actually amuse me to be Lindermann (en route to Anapse) and then—in outfolded style—Anna again. Like a real fold-out girl as from a pornographic magazine. A picture only for your pleasure, a code which only you know the solution.

When you say that the love for A.-over-Avel, now living high up with her blue Beast, has already disappeared when I was in Atepmoc you are lying indeed, my love. To yourself and to me. I remember so clearly myself asking: When did the love story with that woman end? And you answered, very fast and with a sharp sidelong look: Who says it is end?

Thursday night, Negahnepoc.

Mein liebe Liebling, mein Kind und Brüderlein, mein Wirklichkeit und Dicht, mein Angst und Freue, my Arnold—

Just received your letter. Read my "epistle" from Bornholm, remember my new name, and understand that you have done it again, catched me in my heart, beating me in my stomack, taken the air out of my lungs. You have done it again. You have seen me again, seen me as I am (can be), you have lighted me through again, you are a seeing person, seeing me anyway. Oh, Got! I love every word in your letter, letters. A psycoanalist would tear his hair because of your determining of erotic, your picture of me in this fixing-bath, your big tips. I've never met anything like that, you even surpass Ole Holm. I cannot quite recognise myself but if you see me like that, I may be like that, must turn to be like that.

If I'm your breath then you are the very mystery behind the breath, you hit me in the middle, fling everything else overboard so that, terrified and delighted, I see the fine trousseau (embroidered with the wrong initials) float on the sea ("The Rough") for a moment and then go down, disappear. After the real manner of women I think that this anyway was made of by fine linen, could be remade for other purpose. But you laugh —a bit satanic quite frankly—against me with the remains of me between your teeth and my objection blows out of my mouth. My Arnold with what an arrogance you ignore my laborious collected trousseau. Indeed you got me naken. Don't you fear my fury that day the love is worned out. I wrote something for weeks ago after reading 30 pages in Rørvig of Hermann Lobb's *Ein Gesicht* (it was actually written for you,—as everything I think).

So many stories is about "the lust of the flesh and the irreparable loneness of the souls"—you hardly know the quotation, it's from Edews female-poet from about 1900. Now it is only quoted with becoming ironical distance—so many stories about men's loneliness, about men's search for that picture of love which are only given by glimpses. I'm thinking of all the stories (suddenly it seems to me that I never red anything else) about men's effort, their enormous effort in order to give women gifts, to give them their world, builded up through the years, by reading and sensations and meditations and coined in stories told in a floor-bed in Atepmoc or in a tower in old Ebbing or in a grassy field in Adnalri, old wetland of obelisks and follies. All this you give away for a kiss. But when a woman reads these stories, hears that music, she knows them in another direction, sees another message too, she sees her presents in their tenderness and beauty as demands. This gifts demands her "obliteration." She must follow the man in his world, let her be drowned in presents, follow the man in his dreams, make his dreams alive, turn herself into his dreams. And she knows, she expects—from the very first moment in a new love-meeting—your anger and disappointment, turned into contempt in order to be bearable for yourself. Women are stupid, greedy and self-asserting. Stupid because you, the men, have been thinking everything out, has created everything,—greedy when they are not happy by that they are giveen and self-asserting when they demand their own diffuse univers accepted as real ('Eennab otni Rettil dna' Xes' as we say in Ksnad, meaning that the ilegitimate children of the king are ennobled).

I'm mourning for the love (the creating) that cannot endure. After that follows the lonelisness only useable for telling at that time when the love was there. Towards the loneliness (the disappointment, the end) we are leaded so necessary as to the community (the hope, the beginning). This circle is by most women perceived as created by men, it is him to "blame." She wants to continue the creating of love, prefer to stay in the beginning.

A day that she sees that his touch was casual, that his gifts was not for her, that the love cannot be thought without its cessation, she understands that the love was a lever for something else, something in himself, not her business, something usefull: a new present. From him. Then the beloved woman turns into the un-loved woman, a fearful sign, a fury, a witch or only a tormentor, an envious creature hacking with the rest of her love: the selfishness, the greedyness, the demands. She sees that her contribution (the giving of herself is swallowed, devoured and rise again as something else, something outside her. And she is seized by a deadly hate against this giver who used everything, used her out.

The next time she is offered the love of a man (his world) she sees the shadows from corpses of her sisters and turns into whore, sufrogette or very lonely. Or the most scandalous and most perverse: a woman with the same purpose as a man, a woman excluded from love.

All this, my dear Arnold, I feel in a very strong way in the meeting with you. With my Persiko ("Perversiko" to you) I had not this "problematic" (what a word . .) as you can guess, with him there was a kind of cease-fire, a conspiracy, a looking-at-the-world-together. All the words you can translate to anti-life. With you there are life. I want to live. When I want it enough I will die for it. I love you. I have decided to love you. You made this decision irreversible.

That Joyce conceives women as flot-and jetsam(e) cannot surprise me. He might have forced his women insane, from under the ciro-point, mouldering her in acid (his envie) parted her (his stubborness) catalogued her (his tremendous mind) or put her on nails (his grief). As far as I under-stand Joyce I admire him greatly. I don't think I understand him at all.

Your

Anna

PS: I have a dream this other night about a man whose mouth is filled with gold teeth.

*   *   *

Negahnepoc

Sunday night.

My beloved Arnold,

I like to have letters to my home address. It was not me waiting for hours at the steps, it was the letter. I meant it was 'ynnuf'. I haven't the slightest idea of what the postman looks like. I'm waiting everywhere. And not for hours but always. I remember myself standing on the floor in your bedroom, trying to explain you something. I could not and took a pair of dancing-steps in order to show what I ment. I remember how much it pleased you, this simplicity and joy we had together. To have few words demands clearness in mind. To have many words demands clearness in heart. You easy grows wild. It struck me that in a foreign language you cannot hear if your words are ridiculously, you can only hear your own thoughts. When you send me a sentence like Cioran's I get calm. If I wasn't so damned confused and unconcentrated I would like to study filology. Everything is coined in words (no, all the attempts).

After you put me in the plane in Agalam I've had a time full of missing and turmoil, first a melancholy so I could hardly breathe, then desperation so I could hardly stay in my own skin, then a kind of anger, and then, last, a fear. I've been unsure and disturbed because you never answer that parts of my letters which is not about my erotic feelings for you, I saw (see) it as an evasion of that part of me which try to understand everything happened to me, try to make morales (not necessarily moralities). This 'refusing,' as I called it, hurted me a bit but it does it less and less. Because I love you more and more, focussing myself to love you, to follow you. I see that one must always love by surplus. You have learnt me, my beloved Arnold, to shut up. Well . . . I cannot assert that with all this words, but you have shown me that silence is a possibility, maybe an extraordinary one. No word is so pure as to kiss you ('Enid syk remmelg geg ekki').

. . .

13/7
I have found a possible way to see you in Nodnol. First I bristled by aversion against the thought of Bingo Land in general and Nodnol in particular and the flat there. I had Nilbud and the Slewsub Hotel and Yawlag and the mill and our walkings in the valleys and our accidently guestroom, always, unforgetable, and tender, a little blunt conversation in the evenings with our intellectual host, you and him in fictitious disagreement, your brain-drill, I listening and not listening, and then our (other) drill, invented on the spot, difficult, incalculable, sweetnessing until the uneatable and bitter to the uncognosco with Kurlandic liebewerke like fizzy wine in between with dreadful expanses of doubt and—more dreadfull—emptyness. First I had all this in my mind.

. . .

Volle, das Thema und die neue Technik aus druckende Wirkung erreichen. Pause. Trubes Licht, der Tag hat genau vierzig Watt. So sitzt es mir im Gemut. Forgive me my frankness, my love, my greed. But I must do as you say as long as I have to. I cannot help that. Not now. Early enough I will be myself again.

Now I see myself walking up the steps (you must not come and pick me up, no airport, no taxidrivers, no suitcase-mess. I will not walk in that staircase together with you.) You let the frontdoor unlocked. I go in and put my suitcase in the hall (and lock). You must not come out to me. The way to you I find by following the open doors. I walk around in the flat, you hear me, I'm not coming at once. You are sitting in your working-room (I suppose), sitting in your chair or laying on your bed or swimming on the floor or hanging on the wall. You are in that composing room you have been a hundred times before. The only omen is a rustling which as well could come from a clumsy Poltergeist who anyway is thrown out from society because of its unspiritual noisiness. You still have the last red notes humming in your ear when you feel my lips on your neck. You are surprised. I am there so suddenly as a bee in the Spring, humsing, as you say. There is no transition and not any distance between our absence and presence. The time between the airport in Agalam and our new touch, our repeated touch is only an outer assertion, sweeped off the tablecloth like crumbs. Vanished.

I've feared the silence between us after all this letters, this damned storm of *Dichtung und Wahrheit,* seen it as a stop an emptiness. But it will not be so.

I am looking forward to my Kurlandic Liebewerke and my simple mes-sages, I am looking forward to have no language. I am trustfull both to you and myself, I feel—if I'm listening very much and translate you, not from H'Silgne to Ksnadish, but to the deepest meaning I'm able to see—I feel then maybe I can be a little happy and maybe—who knows—make you a little happy. So your answer can come true: "Iwass senippah ni ouy."

I know you prefer letters with a concrete contents, stories, describtions (best erotical), you want to fill them yourself, yes, put colors on. I send a new cart of Negahnepoc with marks and hidden signs which you can fol-low with the nail of your finger like Job scrabed his wounds with a pot-sherd!

I don't mean it, my Arnold, it's all for your pleasure. Alwas I see in your cheerfulness. Hino cheerfulness. Others may see you otherwise. Not Anna.

. . .

I have imagined my second-coming to Atepmoc un-count times. I should be be more beautifull than you ever saw me before, slight sunburned, my hair a little longer, dressed in a white linen-dress. We wouldt go to Agalam and into our hotel behind the Cathedral, let the-man-in-the-lift take us direct to our room. Then we lock the door and stay wordless on the floor and you kiss me while I stay up the wall and you open my dress while we are kissing each other like mads and I open your cloth and put my hands under your shirt and you will go up in me immedeately and you will come in me nearly just then.

I love you more and more fervently. That you must know. That I must tell you. I don't know it if will do any good for you at all but so it is. You wrote: "I knew you were violent that our love would be difficult." Yes. You are indeed not either the most simple being in this world. Sometimes I'm afraid that you suffer too much. Sometimes you've hinted that you were throught but I don't quite believe you.

My dear, next time ravens visit you then dream then dream, don't fight them follow them until you are witscared yourself and inaccessible for others but not for me. I see the year 1913 and suppose the raven is "a Fallen Eagle" but I prefer my first association. O, I would do that, look at ravens from any possible angle, touch the metallic, cloth fearthers open the yellow bad (and empty) beak and keep the blinking eyes untill one of us looked away.

I'm always thinking of you always missing you, do never anything without imagine you observing me, warming me by your look at it. Often I miss you too bitterly, our long long kiss and your slowly attentive moves inside me and my answers. Other love like rabbits comparing to you. Are rabbits. Only you are my only real man. I miss our butterfly-game, pleasure pleasure and deadly serious and our sombre painfull love I need too, the reverse of pleasure, that which hurted, was nearly impossible. If I was together with you I would cultivate that too, keep us in the painfull. "Reven teg otni a dab Repmet," You once said in the kitchen. Oh no, never

. . .

19. july, daytime.

I'm sick today, have diarré—comical so physical everything must turn— I go into closed doors and have just overturned my coffee all over the desk. I am so weak in hands that I couldn't type if not I knew I could and I couldn't walk if not the walking already was invented.

Strange that you are not afraid at all for a meeting again. I'm so afraid of Nodnol, prefer thousand times Adnalri in October, but I cannot do anything but what you want.

Nodnol. As they say: It's too good to be true. I feel I cannot do anything about it. I don't dare to go into it. Too many 'perhaps,' 'couldt
happen' and 'maybe' around that. As imagination it is extremely loaded.
Gallinaceous. Thanks, my love, for that.

. . .

Yes we should start again in a certain place. I don't know where, not
Negahnepoc. Possibly Bornholm (??). Yawlag I'm thinking of, have been
in all the time, below psycical plans. I think early September will show a
new beauty of Yawlag.
No, I don't think so because I have some money from the State on October 10 because I'm lonely mother (and because of my mad not-paying-
tax-in-all-youth). Do you know that Tax and Honey is the same word in
Ksnadish. Treasure is called so. I guess Treasure covers both, is the
source-word. Well, the Octobre medio I get about 120-Renork notes, —
just for a journey with you. A journey for you. The only thing that dis-
turbs me by the-man-in-the-mill, the lifted mill, is that you don't seem to
know him very well. Isn't it to violence-visit a nice man, drawing an enormous not-english-speaking mistress with you? You decide. I'll come when
you say and where you say.

It troubled me that you could send a letter, before you left so sudden,
without starting: "When can you come back to Atepmoc?" Why only
maybe? and how long time? How could you possibly avoid to respond,
direct, that line? Then I've looked at it from the other side: As a finesse
from you. Any direct reason, any name, would be raw. And a little
wrong. I've choosed the late version. And realized your wisdom. You are
surely right Arnold. You were so often in Atepmoc. And now you are in
Nodnol. My love. I couldt saying nothing then because of the language, I
can say nothing now because of the distance in body and mind. You are
another person. Everything are monologues.

Wrote newly to Gnaw and Sonjaw to say thank you for their kindness
and to Utta and the Pastor in order to say the same. And in order to let
them know, I never forget Atepmoc. Never. Strange so often you mentioned Olé Holm, your instincts are sure, you remind of him, the same
limpid selfishness without any wickedness. He was blond with blue eyes,
you are dark with green eyes, it gives the difference.
Your letter scared me. I know that it will scare me lesser in a couple of
days when I've red it more times. But i know too, that the sight of you and
the dream i dremt after will be lying, always attensive, in the back of my
head. However there is nothing to complaint, I knew it, had expected it,

wondering when it came, I saw it in the very second in Pepinos bar, I saw in your eyes that point where longing and fear are meeting each other. 'Evah a Gniteem'. Strange passionate over-used words.

My scribbling is the same for the moment, I have no other words in this weeks, I look at my "poems" and I'm paralysed with their impossibleness, ridiculousness. "When they come back often enough they become careless," you write. Yes. Like that it is. I presume. I don't know, never reach that distance, am like a child, in it or out of it, burning or forgetting, absorbed or not caring. *My ambitions groan.* Oh yes. That also why I lived so well with you: I had no language to force you into my problems. I became only body and spirit with you. "Dlo ffuts gnignah revo Anna's deah."

I love you, I fear you.

the 23th of July

. . .

Sometimes I have that feeling that we are writing or thinking the same things in the same days, that we are in the same moods in the same periods, I feel how the transport of the letters brings an artificial shifting in the congruence which is presente. A letter arrived: a answer on my own un-mailed letter.

. . .

29. July, in night

Read your letter fast, hunting for love-signs, understood it this night, had a horrific dream now in the very early morning. I've written it down in Ksnadish, show it to you a day we can bear it. Strange strange, I've been catched in such a anxiety on your behalf (an anxiety beside my own) just in that days you went that brain-storming-walk with Cosima. Much more than anxiety, a fearfull danger. Yes. I feel I've invoked it over us, know it is nonsense, you have all the ghosts inside yourself, but maybe I've made them awake. Arnold, what are we going to do? My dream said: The ghosts take over the power, the power you invoked for your own happiness turn against you and swallow you. Like the pearls and the pigs. How do I dare to write to you, to tell you that you must follow the ravens? How do I dare when I must know that it demands a power I dont know if I have? Moreover in my arrogance imagine that I've a strenghts enough for two, for both of us? For you too. Arnold never trust me. Use what you can, never trust me.

• • •

My Knepp was good, very impersonal, I was thinking of nobody, so natural as washing oneself, a ritual, childish nearly. I fucked with the chap twice, it was the bitterness, the bitter need he took. Then I stopped because he approached to me, approached *your* regions. Do you understand? The fucking helped for only a very short time. I put on the amulet again immediatly of course. How can you think I didn't? I only took it off because of delicate reasons.

I meet you in another way than in my former erotic conceptions: lesser touch, more imagination. I tell you, Arnold, I imagine you so would die from it if you were there. I feel you, you are with me, you are in me, you are alive in me, you are flinged up in me, you move in me (slowly and fast) and you die in me, inside me you can stay there and get peace. I tell you, few have been so passionate faithfull to you as I in this months. And I . . . I catch a sweetness so unbearable that I disappear to myself, I dissolve. On the island I found myself on the bed (an afternoon I stealed (stold?) me into my room) laughing against the roof with my face wet by tears.

It is this I don't dare on the beatch because even the smallest help-from-hand is excluded and any other signs from the body.

The feeling of lechery (love too) comes in waves, an indefinite series of stationary waves. From that floating-flowing standstills. The resevoir is filled slowly, the first power from the first wave kept, the next added, all addition and addition untill no more addition is possible.

Exactly so madly I'm thinking of you, of us. I've never met such a absence of barriers from a man before. You must have made your women mad of love when you have been like that to them, too.

NEVER MORE I want to hear who you are fucking at the Third River with the deep smooth vessel. There are so many places in the world, —why the Third River? I fling my sorrow back: Your amulet didn't break or turned in a blaze. I took it off.
You are trembling at the thought of Cosima fucking with Lothar Loop? I understand that. Poor everybody to whom this happen. Was same Cosima trembling when you left her?

Did you son come at Whitsun-time? Do you see Gur and Marr frequently? Are you sometimes talking about me? When do you get up in the morning? What do you eat? When is it dark in the evening and how warm are the days? Here in Dannborg it is very cold, blowing, raining. Are you playing chess alone? Are you sunburned? Do you ever go for walks alone? Have you got a chimney-hat? Tell me about these things, just very short. And other things so I can imagine your days.

Did you love me much the day at the Third River? Really? That day was to me the turn from a loveaffair to love. *Das bad an sich. Das Knepp an sich.*

It is conscious I haven't written about Michaux. I'm sure it will come.

Brüderlein, Do Not Despair,—you had Anapse, now Nodnol, you have your talent for invent things into your music (me to be beautiful, the taste of lemon into transform the omelette, the exhaustion into pleasure)—I only just starting in the magic,—am still on the debet-side, I need you so much.

"My Self" or "Not My Self" as the princess said: You act like you don't understand me when I write: Only selden I was "myself" together with you. You scold me, you persuade me (oh so beautifull beautifull) to real-ize, that 'I was never more muself than when I was with you.' Of course you are right my dear. Of course. *Because* you went so deep there was nearly nothing left from the many years' depositing, many years' habit, style, manners, all that I called "myself," put thus (" ") in order to make you understand.

Indeed you got me naken.

30. july, Negahnepoc.

Knepp means fuck, *the fuck.* You know Kant's famous formulation: *Das Ding an sich* = the thing-in-itself, the reality as it is apart from the dream (our judgement.)

I write you a good telling letter from Bornholm my beloved island (much more than Givrør), next week where I have TIME which is so im-portant as LOVE.

(Bornholm is filled with promises!)

I needed the language both to protect and express my happiness. I needed the language to make hymns to your honour, my love, you who showed me the beauty in the word-less world. But just like it was hard to believe that I was beautifull without cloth—and I was catched by modesty when you unexpected came to the roof—just like that, it was difficult to me to believe, that I was meaningfull without language. Yes, most of all I needed the words to tell you that. I love the language, my own and others, the language as tool, the language which is keeping and effacing, the language you can come to the truth with or be lying with. I needed the words to entertaine you, to amuse you, to put my seal into your heart so you can never forget me.

30 july

Michaux—in Knadish—arrived today. A gift I hardly dared to open.

At last you got me nearly convinced that I was good enough without words, that I was beautifull enough without cloth. The very last time in Cataluna (after 'the sacrificial Kuss') I went out of bed, quite naked, and washed my pussy with a corner of the towel and you observed me from the bed, I smiled at you throug the mirrow and for the first time I was sure that I was beautifull, that I—while I in a accidental hotelroom with a cor- ner of a starched linentowel washed my sex—did something beautifull. How can I go without you? How can you go without me? We don't know each other, no. We exited to a high degree each others' dreams. We don't know each other, we are dreaming. Everything depends on if we are clever to dream. And believe in our dreams. And realize our dreams so fervently we are able to.

That was what I meant by magic.

What did you mean?"

PEARSE HUTCHINSON

Fleadh Cheoil

Subtle capering on a simple thought,
the vindicated music soaring out
each other door in a mean twisting main street,
flute-player, fiddler and penny-whistler
concentrating on one sense only
such a wild elegance of energy gay and sad
few clouds of lust or vanity could form;
the mind kept cool, the heart kept warm;
therein the miracle, three days and nights
so many dances played and so much drinking done,
so many voices raised in singing but none
in anger nor any fist in harm—
Saint Patrick's Day in Cambridge Circus might
have been some other nation's trough of shame.

Hotel-back-room, pub-snug, and large open lounges
made the mean street like a Latin fête,
music for once taking all harm out—
from even the bunting's pathetic blunderings,
and the many mean publicans making money fast,
hand over fat fist, pouring the flat
western porter from black-chipped white enamel,
Dervorgilla's penitent chapel
crumbling arch archaic but east,
only music now releasing her people
like Sweeney's cousins on a branch unable
to find his words, but using music
for all articulateness.

But still the shabby county-town was full,
en fête; on fire with peace—for all

Fleadh cheoil—a festival of music. With the revival of interest in traditional Irish music such festivals have become increasingly popular in the past two decades.

the black-and-white contortionists bred
from black and white enamel ever said.

From Easter Snow and Scartaglin
the men with nimble fingers came
in dowdy Sunday suits,
from Kirkintilloch and Ladbroke Grove came back
in flashy ties and frumpish hats,
to play an ancient music, make it new.
A stranger manner of telling than words can do,
a strange manner, both less and more than words or Bach,
but like, that Whitsuntide, stained-glass in summer,
high noon, rose window, Benedictbeuern pleasure,
and Seán O Neachtain's loving singing wood,
an Nollaig sa tSamhradh.

Owls and eagles, clerks and navvies,
ex-British Tommies in drab civvies,
and glorious-patriots whose wild black brindled hair
stood up for the trench-coats they had no need to wear
that tranquil carnival weekend,
when all the boastful maladies got cured—
the faction-fighting magniloquence,
devoid of charity or amorous sense,
the sun-shunning pubs, the trips to Knock.

One said to me: 'There's heart in that',
pointing at: a thick-set man of middle age,
a thick red drinker's face,
and eyes as bright as good stained-glass,
who played on and on and on
a cheap tin-whistle, as if no race
for petty honours had ever come to pass
on earth, or his race to a stale pass;
tapping one black boot on a white flag,
and us crowding, craning, in at the door,
gaining, and storing up, the heart in that.
With him a boy about eighteen,
tall and thin, but, easy to be seen,

. . . *An Nollaig sa tSamhradh:* Christmas in Summer. From a love-song by Seán
Ó Neachtain, Roscommon-born poet and novelist (1655–1728).

Clare still written all over him
despite his eighteen months among the trim
scaffoldings and grim digs of England;
resting his own tin-whistle for his mentor's riff,
pushing back, with a big red hand, the dank mousy quiff,
turning to me to say, 'You know what I think of it,
over there?
                  Over there, you're free'.
Repeating the word 'free', as gay and sad as his music,
repeating the word, the large bright eyes convinced
of what the red mouth said, convinced beyond
shaming or furtiveness, a thousand preachers,
mothers and leader-writers wasting their breath
on the sweet, foggy, distant-city air.
Then he went on playing as if there never were
either a famed injustice or a parish glare.

                                                    Ennis.

Gaeltacht

Bartley Costello, eighty years old,
sat in his silver-grey tweeds on a kitchen chair,
at his door in Carraroe, the sea only yards away,
smoking a pipe, with a pint of porter beside his boot:
"For the past twenty years I've eaten nothing only
periwinkles, my own hands got them off those rocks.
You're a quarter my age, if you'd stick to winkles
you'd live as long as me, and keep as spry".

In the Liverpool Bar, at the North Wall,
on his way to join his children over there,

The Irish means, in verse 2: "The Irish is less than the water in that glass"; in verse 3: "I speak with strangers. I believe it's right to be speaking with strangers." (Strangers, here, has the sense of outlanders, foreigners, runners-in.) In verse 4: "Ah, son, don't be breaking a boat."

an old man looked at me, then down at his pint
of rich Dublin stout. He pointed at the black glass:
"Is lú í an Ghaeilge ná an t-uisce sa ngloine sin".

Beartla Confhaola, prime of his manhood,
driving between the redweed and the rock-fields,
driving through the sunny treeless quartz glory of Carna,
answered the foreigners' glib pity, pointing at the
small black cows: "You won't get finer anywhere
than those black porry cattle". In a pub near there,
one of the locals finally spoke to the townie:
"Labhraim le stráinséirí. Creidim gur chóir bheith
ag labhairt le stráinséirí". Proud as a man who'd claim:
"I made an orchard of a rock-field,
bougainvillea clamber my turf-ricks".

A Dublin tourist on a red-quarter strand
hunting firewood found the ruins of a boat,
started breaking the struts out—an old man came,
he shook his head and said:
"Áá, a mhac: ná bí ag briseadh báid".

The low walls of rock-fields in the west
are a beautiful clean whitegrey. There are chinks between
the neat stones to let the wind through safe,
you can see the blue sun through them.
But coming eastward in the same county,
the walls grow higher, darkgrey:
an ugly grey. And the chinks disappear:
through those walls you can see nothing.

Then at last you come to the city,
beautiful with salmon basking becalmed black below
a bridge over the pale-green Corrib; and ugly
with many shopkeepers looking down on men like
Bartley Costello and Beartla Confhaola because they
speak in Irish, eat periwinkles, keep
small black porry cattle, and on us
because we are strangers.

Geneva

for Bob Welch

The silver curving fish
upon the shining florin

Bent nearly double as they leant
over the parapet small boys
with home-made tackle caught
in as many minutes five
little silver shining fish
out of the green Rhone.

The silver curving salmon
upon the shining florin

The naked stone horsemen
proud on their tall pediments
flanked the long broad bridge
I watched the intent
excited anglers

An old man with a brown bald head
cried encouragement
and one of the boys who wore
a blue-and-white cap
crimson-tasselled
and clean white socks
crowed non-stop
in a shrill voice:
O ma petite
as the little fish came
swirling up on the line
lost for ever
to the clean green water
O ma petite, ma petite

from *All the Old Gems*

5

One morning your hand raw-looking and swollen; sore. You'd banged it, fisted, over and over, against walls and railings the night before in wild dismay: my greed had betrayed you, my lunacy driven you: "always the soft idiot, softly: me".

We sat beside each other gazing at your hand. I wanted to die, but I couldn't speak; afraid of apology insulting.

"I've got wrinkled knuckles", you said, cheering up a little. As once before I felt the splendor—even the terror—of your power to forgive. So we started trotting out all the old gems.

It reminded me, though, for the first time in years, what it was like to slam a drunken hand against the walls and railings, hitting one's heart, the other's heart, perhaps weeping, stumbling home late.

When you leave this town, I may commit once more that rite of anguish. But may the road rise with you, homeward, blessing can survive the rite of pain: which won't last more than a night or two, for I'll have your gifts to learn, your lessons to enjoy.

I pray to your gods and mine—we share some—to guard you always from the wild rites of the swollen hand, from those who'd harm you into them. Or else to drive you deep into their arms.

And when you've gone I'll kiss my knuckles towards your country, and with any luck all the old gems will come dazzling and somersaulting and ricochetting through the skies from your town to mine, from my town to yours, and once in a blue sun we'll send them back to each other wrapped up in greetings. Thole. Celebrations.

In the morning
Flowering knuckles
When you rise

RICHARD MURPHY

Enigma

Her hair has a sweet smell of girlhood under his face
    Darkening the moon on her pillow.

Tenderly her fingertips probe the furrows of his temple
    And find the questionmark of an ear.

How can she play in the rubble of his pleasure ground
    Paths overgrown with laurel and briar?

How can he pick the fruit she will bear in time to come
    On her lips' not yet flowering bud?

Her future is an apple tree, his past a dark old yew
    Growing together in this orchard now.

Care

Kidded in April above Glencolumbkille
On a treeless hill backing north, she throve
Sucking milk off heather and rock, until

I came with children to buy her. We drove
South, passing Drumcliff. Restless in the car,
Bleating, she gulped at plastic teats we'd shove

Copiously in her mouth. Soon she'd devour
Whatever we'd give. Prettily she poked
Her gypsy head with hornbuds through barbed wire

To nip off pea-tops, her fawn pelt streaked
With Black Forest shadow and Alpine snow.
I stalled her wildness in a pen that locked.

She grew tame and fat, fed on herbs I knew
Her body needed. We ransacked Kylemore
To bring her oakleaf, ivy and bark to chew.

I gutted goatbooks, learning how to cure
Fluke, pulpy kidney, black garget, louping ill:
All my attention bled to cope with her.

No fenceless commonage to roam, no hill
Transfigured into cloud, no dragon wood
To forage with a puck-led flock: but the rattle

Of a bucket, shouts of children bringing food
Across a frozen yard. Out in a forest
She would have known a bad leaf from a good.

Here, captive to our taste, she'd learnt to trust
The petting hand with crushed oats, or a new
Mash of concentrates, or sweet bits of waste.

So when a child mistook a sprig of yew
And mixed it with her fodder, she descried
No danger: we had tamed her instinct too.

Whiskey, white of egg, linseed oil, we tried
Forcing down antidotes. Nothing would do.
The children came to tell me when she died.

Swallows

She wades through wet rushes,
Long autumn grass,
Over rusty barbed wire
And stone walls that collapse,

With a black rubber torch
That keeps flickering off,
After midnight, to reach
A shed with a tin roof.

She lifts away door-boards—
O sweet herbal hay!
Her beam dazzles birds
She can't identify.

Timorous wings in wormy rafters
Flap to get out.
Then she spots in a light-shaft
A red boot unlaced.

The flock's tremor increases
In her torch's coop.
Where is he? She sees
A white arm sticking up.

Trouvaille

This root of bog-oak the sea dug up she found
Poking about, in old age, and put to stand
Between a snarling griffin and a half-nude man
Moulded of lead on my chimney-piece.
It looks like a heron rising from a pond,
Feet dipped in brown-trout water,
Head shooting arrow-sharp into blue sky.

"What does it remind you of?" she wanted to know.
I thought of trees in her father's demesne
Levelled by chainsaws;
Bunches of primroses I used to pick
Before breakfast, hunting along a limestone lane,
To put at her bedside before she woke;
And all my childhood's broken promises.

No, no! It precedes alphabets,
Planted woods, or gods.
Twisted and honed as a mind that never forgets
It lay dead in bog acids, undecayable:
Secretively hardening in a womb of moss, until
The peat burnt off, a freak tide raised
The feathered stick she took to lure me home.

Mary Ure

Bare feet she dips across my boat's blue rail
In the ocean as we run under full white summer sail.
The cold spray kisses them. She's not immortal.

Sitting in her orchard she reads *Lady Lazarus*
Aloud rehearsing, when her smallest child lays
Red peonies in her lap with tender apologies.

She walks by Lough Mask in a blue silk gown
So thin the cloudy wind is biting to the bone
But she talks as lightly as if the sun shone.

The Price of Stone

How much it hurts me to tidy up when all my papers are
    heaped on the desk in a three-month mess,
To regain control of this drift of days I've lost in
    my passion for building in granite,
And face the bills I must pay by leaving the house
    that has cost me too much to enlarge,
Where I passed the time too quickly preparing a place for
    the future to work within soundproof walls,

So never had a moment in the present for writing about
    the moments that were passing away:
How much it hurts to see the destruction that all good
    building, even the best, must cause,
Not only the hedges that had to be first cut down
    before the foundations were dug,
But deeper cuts through veins in the mind that carried
    the blood of memory through the brain:
How much it hurts me to have neglected all this summer
    the friends whom I might have seen,
But for my mad obsession of building more rooms
    to entertain them in time to come:
Because these times are apt to elude us, we die, or our
    friends drop dead before we can say
I'd love you to see and enjoy the house whose construction
    has kept us entirely apart.

THOMAS KINSELLA

Finistère

I . . .
One . . .

I smelt the weird Atlantic.
Finistère . . .

           Finisterre . . .

The sea surface darkened. The land behind me,
and all its cells and cysts, grew dark.
From a bald boulder on the cairn top
I spied out the horizon to the northwest
and sensed that minute imperfection again.
Where the last sunken ray withdrew . . .
A point of light?

A maggot of the possible
wriggled out of the spine
into the brain.

We hesitated before that wider sea
but our heads sang with purpose
and predatory peace.
And whose excited blood was that
fumbling our movements? Whose ghostly hunger
tunnelling our thoughts full of passages
smelling of death ash and clay and faint metals
and great stones in the darkness?

The origin and some details of "Finisté" and "The Oldest Place" derive from *Lebor Gabála Érenn* (The Book of the Conquests of Ireland), a medieval compilation which synchronised early Irish cosmogonic myths with the Church's established Biblical temporal schema and posited the genesis of the Irish race in a series of invasions, each of which left more clearly defined territories and tribes behind it.

At no great distance out in the bay
the swell took us into its mercy,
grey upheaving slopes of water
sliding under us, collapsing,
crawling onward, mountainous.

Driven outward a day and a night
we held fast, numbed by the steady
might of the oceanic wind.
We drew close together, as one,
and turned inward, salt chaos
rolling in silence all around us,
and listened to our own mouths
mumbling in the sting of spray:
—Ill wind end well
  mild mother
  on wild water pour peace

  who gave us our unrest
  whom we meet and unmeet
  in whose yearning shadow
  we erect our great uprights
  and settle fulfilled
  and build and are still
  unsettled, whose goggle gaze
  and holy howl we have scraped
  speechless on slabs of stone
  poolspirals opening on
  closing spiralpools
  and dances drilled in the rock
  in coil zigzag angle and curl
  river ripple earth ramp
  suncircle moonloop . . .
  in whose outflung service
  we nourished our hunger
  uprooted and came

  in whale hell

                gale gullet

  salt hole

                dark nowhere

calm queen

     pour peace

The bad dream ended at last.
In the morning, in a sunny breeze,
bare headlands rose fresh out of the waves.
We entered a deep bay, lying open
to all the currents of the ocean.
We were further than anyone had ever been
and light-headed with exhaustion and relief
—three times we misjudged and were nearly driven
on the same rock.
               (I had felt all this before . . .)
We steered in along a wall of mountain
and entered a quiet hall of rock echoing
to the wave-wash and our low voices.
I stood at the prow. We edged to a slope of stone.
I steadied myself. 'Our Father . . .', someone said
and there was a little laughter. I stood
searching a moment for the right words.
They fell silent. I chose the old words once more
and stepped out. At the solid shock
a dreamy power loosened at the base of my spine
and uncoiled and slid up through the marrow.
A flow of seawater over the rock fell back
with a she-hiss, plucking at my heel.
My tongue stumbled

Who
    is a breath
that makes the wind
that makes the wave
that makes   this   voice?

Who
    is the bull with seven scars
the hawk on the cliff
the salmon sunk in his pool
the pool sunk in her soil
the animal's fury
the flower's fibre
a teardrop in the sun?

Who
        is the word that spoken
the spear springs
        and pours out terror
the spark springs
        and burns in the brain?

When men meet on the hill
dumb as stones in the dark
        (the craft knocked behind me)
who is the jack of all light?
Who goes in full into
the moon's interesting conditions?
Who fingers the sun's sink hole?
        (I went forward, reaching out)

The Oldest Place

We approached the shore. Once more.
                                Repeated memory
shifted among the green-necked confused waves.
The sea wind and spray tugged and refreshed us,
but the stale reminder of our sin still clung.

We would need to dislodge
the flesh itself, to dislodge that
—shrivel back to the first drop
and be spat back shivering into
the dark beyond our first father.

                        *

We fished and fowled and chopped at the forest,
cooked and built, ploughed and planted,
danced and drank, all as before.
But worked inland, and got further.
And there was something in the way the land behaved:
passive, but responding. It grew under our hands.

We worked it like a dough to our requirements
yet it surprised us more than once
with a firm life of its own, as if
it used us.
              Once, as we were burying
one of our children, the half-dug grave
dampened, and overbrimmed, and the water
ran out over the land and would not stop
until the place had become a lake.

*

Year followed year.
The first skin blemishes appeared,
and it almost seemed we had been waiting for them.
The sickness and the dying began again.

To make things easier, we decided
to come together in one place.
We thought of the bare plain we found first,
with the standing stone: miles of dead clay
without a trace of a root or a living thing.
We gathered there and the sick died
and we covered them. Others fell sick
and we covered them, fewer and fewer.
A day came when I fell down by the great stone
alone, crying, at the middle of the stinking plain.

*

Night fell, and I lay there face down,
and I dreamed that my ghost stood up
and faint starry shadows everywhere
lifted themselves up and began
searching about among themselves for something,
hesitant at first, but quickly certain,
and all turning
              —muscular nothingnesses,
demons, animal-heads, wrestling vaguely toward me
reaching out terrible gifts into my face,
clawfuls of dripping cloth
and gold and silver things.
They passed through me. . .

                        To the stone,
and draped it with their gifts, murmuring,
and dropped them about its base.
With each gift, the giver
sighed and melted away,
the black stone packed more
with dark radiance.

                And I dreamed
that my ghost moved toward it, hand on heart,
the other hand advanced. . .
                        And its glare
gathered like a pulse, and struck
on the withered plain of my own brain.

                        *

A draped black shaft under the starlight,
with bars and blocks and coils of restless metal
piled about it, and eyes hovering
above those abnormal stirrings.
A little higher, where there might have been branches,
a complex emptiness shimmered in front of the stars.

A shawl shifted on the top, dangled
black and silver, a crumpled face
with forehead torn crisscross, begging,
with tongue flapping, *Agath, Kak,*
and dropped to earth.

JOHN MONTAGUE

Dowager

I dwell in this leaky Western castle.
American matrons weave across the carpet,
Sorefooted as camels, and less useful.

Smooth Ionic columns hold up a roof.
A chandelier shines on a foxhound's coat:
The grandson of a grandmother I reared.

In the old days I read or embroidered,
But now it is enough to see the sky change,
Clouds extend or smother a mountain's shape.

Wet afternoons I ride in the Rolls;
Windshield wipers flail helpless against the rain:
I thrash through pools like smashing panes of glass.

And the light afterwards! Hedges steam,
I ride through a damp tunnel of sweetness,
The bonnet strewn with bridal hawthorn

From which a silver lady leaps, always young.
Alone, I hum with satisfaction in the sun,
An old bitch, with a warm mouthful of game.

The Errigal Road

We match paces along the Hill Head Road,
the road to the old churchyard of Errigal Keerogue;
its early cross, a heavy stone hidden in grass.

As we climb, my old Protestant neighbour
signals landmarks along his well trodden path,
some hill or valley celebrated in local myth.

'Yonder's Whiskey Hollow', he declares,
indicating a line of lunar birches.
We halt to imagine men plotting

against the wind, feeding the fire or
smothering the fumes of an old fashioned worm
while the secret liquid bubbles & clears.

'And that's Foxhole Brae under there—'
pointing to the torn face of a quarry.
'It used to be crawling with them.'

(A red quarry slinks through the heather,
a movement swift as a bird's, melting as rain,
glimpsed behind a mound, disappears again.)

At Fairy Thorn Height the view fans out,
ruck and rise to where, swathed in mist
& rain, swells the mysterious saddle shape

of Knockmany Hill, its brooding tumulus
opening perspectives beyond our Christian myth.
'On a clear day you can see far into Monaghan,'

old Eagleson says, and we exchange sad notes
about the violence plaguing these parts;
last week, a gun battle outside Aughnacloy,

machine gun fire splintering the wet thorns,
two men beaten up near dark Altamuskin,
an attempt to blow up Omagh Courthouse.

Helicopters overhead, hovering locusts.
Heavily booted soldiers probing vehicles, streets,
their strange antennae bristling, like insects.

At his lane's end, he turns to face me.
'Tell them down South that old neighbours
can still speak to each other around here'

& gives me his hand, but does not ask me in.
Rain misting my coat, I turn back towards
the main road, where cars whip smartly past

between small farms, fading back into forest.
Soon all our shared landscape will be effaced,
a quick stubble of pine recovering most.

Caught

A slight girl and easily got rid of:
He took his pleasure in an idle dance,
Laughed to hear her cry under him,
But woke to find his body in a trance.
Wherever he walked, he seemed to see
Her approaching figure, whoever spoke
He strained for echoes of her voice,
And, in a rage of loss, turned back
To where she slept, hands clasped on
Small breasts in a posture of defence.
Conqueror turned plaintiff, he tries
To uncurl them, to see long-lashed eyes
Turn slowly up, hear a meek voice say:
'Are you back, my love, back to stay?'

Pastourelle

Hands on the pommel,
long dress trailing
over polished leather
riding boots, a spur
jutting from the heel,
& beneath, the bridle path,
strewn with rusty apples,
brown knobs of chestnut,
meadow saffron and acorn.

Then we were in the high
ribbed dark of the trees
where animals move stealth-
ily, coupling & killing,
while we talked nostalgically
of our lives, bedevilled
& betrayed by lost love—
the furious mole, tunnelling
near us his tiny kingdom—

& how slowly we had come
to where we wished each other
happiness, far and apart, as
a hawk circled the wood,
& a victim cried, the sound
of hooves rising & falling
upon bramble & fern, while
a thin growth of rain gathered about us, like a cowl.

Herbert Street Revisited

for Madeleine

I

A light is burning late
in this Georgian Dublin street:
someone is leading our old lives!

And our black cat scampers again
through the wet grass of the convent garden
upon his masculine errands.

The pubs shut: a released bull,
Behan shoulders up the street,
topples into our basement, roaring 'John!'

A pony and donkey cropped flank
by flank under the trees opposite;
short neck up, long neck down,

as Nurse Mullen knelt by her bedside
to pray for her lost Mayo hills,
the bruised bodies of Easter Volunteers.

Animals, neighbours, treading the pattern
of one time and place into history,
like our early marriage, while

tall windows looked down upon us
from walls flushed light pink or salmon
watching and enduring succession.

II

As I leave, you whisper,
'don't betray our truth'
and like a ghost dancer,
invoking a lost tribal strength
I halt in tree-fed darkness

to summon back our past,
and celebrate a love that eased
so kindly, the dying bone,
enabling the spirit to sing
of old happiness, when alone.

III

So put the leaves back on the tree,
put the tree back in the ground,
let Brendan trundle his corpse down
the street singing, like Molly Malone.

Let the black cat, tiny emissary
of our happiness, streak again
through the darkness, to fall soft
clawed into a landlord's dustbin.

Let Nurse Mullen take the last
train to Westport, and die upright
in her chair, facing a window
warm with the blue slopes of Nephin.

And let the pony and donkey come—
look, someone has left the gate open—
like hobbyhorses linked in
the slow motion of a dream

parading side by side, down
the length of Herbert Street,
rising and falling, lifting
their hooves through the moonlight.

JOHN JORDAN

Passion

THEY ARRIVED IN SEVILLE at six o'clock in the evening and Dympna was tired after the five-hour bus ride from Algeciras. She complained also of a pain in her tummy. Bill sympathized with her fatigue and her pain and bore with her small moans and injured eyes. He loved his wife. What completely staggered him was her request for a cup of tea.

For three weeks she had been admirable and Bill had been proud of her. Not once had she complained about the food or the water or the lavatories, and Bill's happiness was increased by the knowledge that his wife—his Dympna—was sophisticated enough to take the rough with the smooth in foreign travel. Sometimes in the middle of the night when Dympna had gone asleep and he lay awake sweating under their single sheet, he would make up fantasies about their future married life: Dympna and himself mastering Western Europe, summer after glittering summer, coming back to Dublin year after year with stories to dazzle the chaps in the office and Dympna's girl-friends. But as the light dripped through the slats, Bill would catch himself on, for there must and should be children, and he thanked God, in manly fervour, for this wonderful honeymoon.

The cup of tea worried him. Bill had muddled notions about conforming to the customs of the country, and he felt it would be a betrayal of them both to ask for a cup of tea. But when they were settled in their *pensión de lujo*, which cost a bit more but was worth it, Dympna's pain went and she perked up and no more was heard about the cup of tea. She even hummed to herself while they were washing and changing, and Bill would have liked to look round, but of course did not do so, for after three weeks of marriage they both retained their modesty.

And Dympna looked quite lovely when they went down to dinner, her corn-coloured hair swept back, and her thin-honed shoulders sloping red-brown out of her flared blue cotton. When Bill caught a glimpse of himself in one of the mirrors on the staircase, he thought that he too looked good, with a nice parting in his reddish hair and a smooth tan and a snow-white shirt. You had to hand it to the Spaniards, they got things really white.

When they got to the first turn in the staircase that led to the big roofed *patio,* they almost collided with a young Spaniard. There were bows and retreats and steppings-aside and apologies, and the Spaniard, a smudge of black and olive and white, smiled with what even Bill had to recognise as charm. Dympna's flush came and lingered under her sunburn, and Bill, though proud of being an Irishman, found himself thinking, like a story-book Englishman, that the fellow was too good-looking to be healthy.

In the *patio* other guests were getting up to go in to the dining-room. They were mostly French students, plain, noisy, enthusiastic boys and girls. During the meal they had complicated and fatuous arguments about the temperature of the water, the difference between French and Spanish oils, what they should do and where they should go the day after.

Bill half-listened to them, for though Dympna ate almost greedily and drank more wine than usual, she said nothing beyond 'Pass the salt, please,' and 'This fish is good,' and Bill thought suddenly that they might as well be two strangers seated by chance at the same table. The thought came like a cramp.

'A peach for *la señora?*'

'*Sí, sí.*'

For the first time Bill failed to respond with joy and astonishment to the phrase which more than 'Mrs.' or 'Madame' seemed to establish his new possession and his new way of life. He poured more wine and thought, 'It's too soon, God, it's too soon.' Around him swelled the din of the French, as the roar of traffic might reach a patient in a hospital.

It was half-past ten when they finished dinner. Bill asked Dympna if she'd like to take a stroll and have some coffee. She said she was tired and would like to go to bed.

Each new town they had come to, they had wandered a little on the first night. They had sniffed the mystery of a two- or three-day home, inspecting cafés and marking down itineraries, cherishing an unexpected silhouette or a companionable bell. And now in Seville it was different.

Bill was as silent and as nervous as Dympna as they undressed for bed. To-night she did not ask him to brush her hair and he did not ask her to scratch his back, a service which had begun as an urgent request and continued as the first joke of married life.

Bill stood at the window a moment before drawing the heavy Venetian blind. He could see below him across the way through an open window, some Negro boys sitting around a gramophone. He had forgotten about Spain's colonials. In their happy exile they played old-fashioned popular tunes of the 'forties. Now it was 'Moonlight becomes you'. The faded melody, defiant in the city of Moor and Jew and Christian, made Bill feel tearful and self-pitying and full of desire. Dympna was in bed now, her hair dull yellow against the pillow, and lying as she always did while she waited for him, like an effigy on a tomb. As he turned fully towards her Bill was shocked by the keenness of his desire and his sick tenderness. Not even a husband had a right to feel like this. 'Men, you must learn to master your passions': the comedian's Cork accent barracked in his ears and at the back of his nostrils was the attar of incense and body-sweat.

She drew away from him. This had happened twice before, once for reasons he imperfectly understood but which he accepted as normal and once because he had gone off drinking with an American and come back smelling like a wine-shop. Otherwise she had understood the requirements of his love, for he was not, as a rule, hot-blooded. Now he lay on his back beside her and wondered what was wrong. He watched the shadows on the ceiling, and felt the sweat working down his spine, and his desire and tenderness dwindled into lust and petulance that might have been consoled anywhere.

The Negroes continued to play their sweet stale tunes, and the bells of midnight began to perform, silver after silver, gold after gold, and then what must be the imperial decent bronze of the Cathedral.

And then after the confusion of the bells, Bill thought that he was having delusions. He imagined he heard 'The Londonderry Air' played on a trumpet. But he realized it must be another record from across the way. As the trumpet yearned to the top notes, Bill's eyes began to smart and he reached out his hand to Dympna. She did not move.

The shadows were losing ground on the ceiling. He thought about other shadows: the chestnut tree on the lawn where he first kissed her, jumping fire-light when he proposed to her, the watery moon in the Left Bank hotel room . . . He looked at his watch. It was half-past one. Dympna seemed to be asleep.

He got up quietly and groped his way to his hold-all. He rummaged until he found the flask of cognac which he had not touched since Paris. He felt as he had not felt since he first stayed out all night at home, and crept back to safety before light. Guilty, exultant, chilled.

After the first slug he became a little weepier. 'Christ,' he thought, 'what makes it worse, you can't even get drunk in Spain.' And he felt homesick for the chaps in the office and the stag binges and the squalid half-virgin fumblings with ginny girls. He slugged again. A warm, safe, untidy world, and a damned sight better than standing half-naked in a Spanish hotel-room, swilling cognac furtively while your unfriendly wife slept or pretended to sleep in your marriage bed.

He realized that he had finished the bottle and groped his way back to the bed. He tossed and thumped until Dympna thought he would never stop and then, suddenly, he dropped asleep, as the bull drops dead.

She could, by turning her head slightly, see the outlines of his jaw and a shadow of hair, and a glisten of sweat on his chest where his jacket had fallen open, and she smelt the cognac from his breath. She stretched out her hand, then drew it back. Slowly, laboriously, like an infant being rehearsed by the nuns, she made the Sign of the Cross. She twisted her left elbow so as not to disturb Bill.

For the fifth time that night she prayed for strength against temptation, telling on her fingers the Sorrowful Mysteries, meditating as best she could on the Agony, the Scourging, the Crowning and the Carrying. She had reached the Crucifixion when her sore eye-lids gave up the ghost. She fell asleep before the image of a young Spaniard on a Cross, all black and olive and white except for the purple at the hands and feet and side. In her dreams she kissed the feet, and covered them with her corn-coloured hair.

EUGENE McCABE

from *King of the Castle*

TRESSA: Barney?

SCOBER: Yes.

TRESSA: Nothing.

SCOBER: Go on daughter . . . go on.

TRESSA: Are you happy?

SCOBER: Am I happy?

TRESSA: Yes?

SCOBER: Well,? Yes . . . most ways . . . tethered a bit maybe . . .times I'd as leif have less . . . milk, a cow or two . . . up early to dig or gather the day long . . . bone tired at duskus . . . eat and drink like a horse . . . sleep sound . . . it's never that way: Rain when you wake . . . a toothache maybe or a cold . . . or your head's light from whiskey or you've been vexed from half-dark with cares . . . or up half the night at figures . . . coming or going; docks, marts; money to make! the day never comes when you do the things you as leif do . . . it's most times things you'd as leif not do . . . [*Pause*] . . . but . . . happy? Happy I'd say as any man . . . why?

TRESSA: Just.

SCOBER: Just what?

TRESSA: Do you love me Barney? Please look at me . . . do you?

SCOBER: You jump things on me woman. . . . Am I happy? Do I love you? . . . words, respect is better.

TRESSA: I say them.

SCOBER: Respect is better.

TRESSA: You don't understand. . . .

SCOBER: Too well

[*Long Pause*]

TRESSA: He doesn't respect you.

SCOBER: Who?

TRESSA: Maguire.

SCOBER: He's jealous—That's respect . . . jealous, 'cause I've worked—
used my head—put lorries on the road—got this place and others—
bought out most of the mountain—planted timber, built barns,
roofed yards—I employ men—I have a young wife. . . . [*Pause
pointing up*] Electric . . . [*Longish pause*] I was in rags at school
with all of them—but you've got to stay that way—raggy, stupid
and poor—"Ah! sure it's a hard life" and "How can a man live where
snipes starve?" "But won't we get our reward afterwards?"—
slobber!! [*Pointing out*] There's ton of barley to the acre from three
inches of soil out there—stones, a lot of it—and there's men in
Meath on the fattest land in Ireland'd lie happy with a yield like
that, and still the fools'd starve before they'd ask "How's it done?"
"Can I do it?"—Spite! Ignorance! Envy. Let 'em starve—let 'em live
on spite and take the boat—rotten thatch with lumps of grass—all
sunk away from the chimneys—windows that leave it dusk inside of
a Summer's day—the dungheap and the bony cow—the messy yard
and the few mousey sheep—I was born to it—know every hour of it
—the waste, the crownshawning by the fire in Winter. Everything
to blame but themselves and cause they don't do anything—like
Maguire, they've time to watch—every turf you save and lamb you
mark—the lorries that come and go—they count and question and
what they don't know they guess, and if man improves—they say:
—"No man bests the mountain less he's a thief like Bull Haggard."
But if you work and deal and best the mountain—you've made *dirt*
of them—and that's what they hate—order—yields—business, the
power to buy. . . .

TRESSA: [*Remotely*] For what?

SCOBER: Eh?!

TRESSA: I said for what?

SCOBER: How do you mean—?

TRESSA: All this buying—what's it for?

[*Pause*]

SCOBER: Us. [*Pause while Scober reflects*] Hundreds of years—we've
scraped those rocks—The grave-yards full of McAdams—Tobins—
Mullarkeys—lived and died—lek scarecrows. When I was a cub I
could see this place—these windows lit up like a ship now I look out
of them. . . .

TRESSA: At neighbours . . . you've bought out—at nothing. I'm listening
now three years—you go on and on and on Barney—talking to

yourself—power—the mountain—spite and the neighbours—Soon we'll have no neighbours—We don't even fit it right. . . .

SCOBER: We can afford it. . . .

TRESSA: Not enough. . . .

SCOBER: If you can pay for a thing—you fit it.

TRESSA: [*Unlistening*] Those people last week. . . .

SCOBER: To Hell with them.

[*Pause*]

TRESSA: What I didn't say was what she said when I opened the door [*Pause*] I'd an apron on—she asked—very nicely: was there *anybody* at home. . . . [*Scober reacts with annoyance*] So I said no . . . what could I say when they thought I worked here. They wanted to see round the place the house and garden—she had spent holidays here with her aunts—did I think the present owners would mind. "No," I said, "it's all right," and I went back to the kitchen.

SCOBER: This means what?

TRESSA: We don't fit it. . . .

SCOBER: An empty barracks with no roof when I got it—laurel branches through that window there—now look. . . .

[*Tressa looks up without interest*]

TRESSA: [*Pause*] It doesn't leak—it's wrong every other way. . . .

[*Scober stares*]

SCOBER: We've spent money on it but—it's wrong—it should be different —How?!

TRESSA: Don't shout Barney. . . . [*Pause*] Take our dump room off the hall, it used to be a library—the shelving's still there. . . . My first week here I counted how many books went round the walls [*Pause*] . . . Guess. . . . [*Scober shrugs with annoyance*] Five thousand.

SCOBER: I'd prefer bank notes—you can buy bread with them. . . .

TRESSA: That's why we've none.

SCOBER: So. . . . !?

TRESSA: So—it's different now—we keep worm doses, cod liver oil, farming papers, syringes, pig powders—and twenty years of Old Moore's Almanac, where there used to be five thousand books— women in long dresses—candle light—wine—a big log fire.

SCOBER: 'S not so long since we were growled at by gun dogs—and handed gruel in workhouses, those with no pride—the rest stayed hungry— or left in coffin ships and died—by the million. . . . If I've a sick pig —I want a pig powder, a syringe and farming papers, not some book about some knucks who don't matter any more. Anyway they're dyin'—all over the country—places like this. . . . It's starin' at them—a slate here and there—a few acres now and then—pressure —change—thirty—fifty years—that's all they've got—and men who understand how to buy and sell—who understand land and stock—move in—not for mouldy books, log fires—or wine. . . .

TRESSA: [*Muttered*] To squeeze out "their own". . . .

SCOBER: For work!

TRESSA: For nothing. . . .

SCOBER: [*Ironically*] Must have been the way you were reared—this taste for the old style. . . .

TRESSA: *Living*, Barney—living. . . .

SCOBER: The homeplace—this bungalow your brothers built from a six-penny plan—did you *live* over there. . . . [*Pause*] Plan must have said nothing about the dungheap . . . looks tidy outside the kitchen door—nice concrete walls, but. . . .

TRESSA: [*Drily*] I was in Dublin when they built that.

SCOBER: I'd say. . . . Couldn't see a book the last time I was there—A Sacred Heart and the Butcher's Calendar on the kitchen wall—that's the only style I saw. I wouldn't mind—only I gave you a free hand three years ago. [*Tressa nods impatiently*] Near a thousand pounds —that's what it was for paint and paper.

TRESSA: What's that when we end up with this—people who know about it think it silly—

SCOBER: What *people*?!

TRESSA: The goldy wallpaper—the shiny lino—the prints—this bedroom stuff—

SCOBER: What *people*?

TRESSA: The ones last week. [*Pause*] Know what he said? "Hideous"— "Truly hideous," and then she said, "I'd rather see it empty, open to the sky". . . .

SCOBER: I saw them. . . . Who are they? He looked lek a man with a corkscrew up his arse, and she looked worried about it—Next time put the dog on them—I like it this way—the way you done it. [*He looks round the walls and ceiling: shrugs*] If you don't like it now—We'll change it sometime. . . .

TRESSA: I don't give a damn about it. . . .

SCOBER: [*Nonplussed*] No!? Why all this whine . . . there's somethin'— what—?

TRESSA: *He* came back. . . .
SCOBER: *Who* came back?
TRESSA: Maguire. . . .

[*Pause*]

SCOBER: Here?

[*Tressa nods*]

TRESSA: His cap—he said. . . .
SCOBER: [*Tensely*] Well. . . . ?

[*Long pause*]

TRESSA: He said—he saw you—years back: in a bad house. . . . [*Scober reacts to this more with hatred of Maguire than shame*] Were you Barney? [*Scober shrugs*] With other women? [*Scober stares*] You told me I was the. . . .
SCOBER: You're young. . . .
TRESSA: Were you?
SCOBER: You don't understand. . . .
TRESSA: You lied.
SCOBER: When you were born I was older'n you are now. . . .
TRESSA: I believed you. . . .
SCOBER: It was a poor question . . . and you?
TRESSA: What?
SCOBER: You? [*Tressa stares suddenly distracted and embarrassed: Pause*] That's right: say nothin'—I'm a bit old for stories—What else?
TRESSA: [*Embarrassed and angry*] What?!
SCOBER: 'Bout Maguire?
TRESSA: [*Sharply*] I don't know—He talked in riddles.
SCOBER: 'Bout me? . . . .
TRESSA: And me. . . .
SCOBER: What does he know 'bout you?
TRESSA: He can guess well—[*Pause*] "What's a woman for," he said "scrapes plates—twig floors, look at rocks and heather" [*Looking back at Scober*] "To drain a man and rear a man". . . .
SCOBER: [*Almost in a whisper*] He said that?
TRESSA: More—he said—"Take me, I'm a man I'll put a belly on you."
SCOBER: [*Incredulous*] You made that up?!
TRESSA: He said it. . . .

[Long pause]

SCOBER: "Put a belly on you". . . .

TRESSA: *[Deadpan]* That's what he said. . . . *[Muttered]*—Maybe he could too. *[Pause]* You stand there as if nothing's happened—and. . . .

SCOBER: *[With a great effort at control]* Nothin' did. . . .

TRESSA: You don't care. . . .

SCOBER: Why tell me this?

TRESSA: Because it happened.

SCOBER: Awhile back we made a deal—no talk—no half-talk—and you said *[Loud]* Alright—and every day since—you give the jag,—your time—last night—Maguire—to-day. . . .

TRESSA: I told you because. . . .

SCOBER: 'Reminded' me—because . . . *[Pause]* to-morrow—you'll let me know your time's up—the next day you're bitchy, the next itchy. . . . You should travel with me and listen in—*You suffer*—"How's all the care, Scober?"—"Any more on that woman of yours?" "You want a *man* about the house." I listen and when they smile, I smile: when they laugh, I laugh, if a man's deaf—he's deaf. . . .

TRESSA: You don't want to hear. . . .

SCOBER: Hear what?

TRESSA: What you know. . . . *[Pause]*

SCOBER: *[Tensely]* Say it! *[Pause]* *[Louder]* Say it! . . . .

TRESSA: You say it Barney . . . you're not a proper man. . . . *[Scober walks away: Tressa goes to him]*

JAMES SIMMONS

What Will You Do, Love?

'What will you do, love, when ambition presses
and from your caresses
I fly away?
Obliged to sever, I wonder whether
we'll feel together
day after day?'

'When I am alone and you are the apple
of the eyes of people
beyond my view,
I'll pray that praise will never destroy you,
I'll wait to enjoy you.
That's what I'll do.'

'What will you do, with concerts flopping
and no one clapping
your husband there?
If nerves or drink or rich fools tempt me
and my wallet's empty,
love, will you care?'

'If you come to bore me with a bad luck story,
love, I'll ignore ye
or break your head;
but, poor and pale, if it's honest failure
I'll see what ails you
and warm your bed.'

'And if in the nubile girls of fashion
I find a passion
that makes me stay,
what will you do if I deceive you
and want to leave you
and stay away?'

'The usual thing: with my young heart aching
but never breaking
I'll think of you;
but the wounds will heal, and when grief is over
I'll love some other.
That's what I'll do.'

Cavalier Lyric

I sometimes sleep with other girls
in boudoir or cheap joint,
with energy and tenderness
trying not to disappoint.
So do not think of helpful whores
as aberrational blots;
I could not love you half so well
without my practice shots.

The End of the Affair

We could count the times we went for a walk
Or the times we danced together in the past
Months—if not the times of making love and talk.
Our first separation will be our last.

I suppose we never discussed what we have known:
That I am to go home, that you will stay.
All the mutual tenderness that has grown,
Sweet as it is, is not to get in the way

Of the work before us, mine and yours.
What has been given is being taken away,
And we aren't looking for loopholes and cures,
Freely absenting ourselves from this felicity

To tell our story under plain covers
In bed, or by example, till everyone understands
That joy will not be bound. Artists and lovers
Start and complete their work with empty hands.

To leave my wife and children for love's sake
And marry you would be a failure of nerve.
I remember love and all that goes to make
The marriage, the affairs, that I deserve.

Stephano Remembers

We broke out of our dream into a clearing
and there were all our masters still sneering.
My head bowed, I made jokes and turned away,
living over and over that strange day.

The ship struck before morning. Half past four,
on a huge hogshead of claret I swept ashore
like an evangelist aboard his god:
his will was mine, I laughed and kissed the rod,
and would have walked that foreign countryside
blind drunk, contentedly till my god died;
but finding Trinculo made it a holiday:
two Neapolitans had got away,
and that shipload of scheming toffs we hated
was drowned. Never to be humiliated
again, 'I will no more to sea,' I sang.
Down white empty beaches my voice rang,
and that dear monster, half fish and half man,
went on his knees to me. Oh, Caliban,
you thought I'd take your twisted master's life;
but a drunk butler's slower with a knife
than your fine courtiers, your dukes, your kings.
We were distracted by too many things . . .
the wine, the jokes, the music, fancy gowns.
We were no good as murderers, we were clowns.

THOMAS KILROY

from *Talbot's Box*

PRIEST FIGURE: Oh, a fine man, Mr. Mac. A credit to his country.

TALBOT: And what do they mane, father, be the word cat-cat-cat-a-lep-tic?

PRIEST FIGURE: [*Standing behind*] It means, Matt, being in a kind of state, in a kind of trance, you might say. Doctors use it.

TALBOT: Is that so? [*Chuckle*] When ya think of the words they need!

PRIEST FIGURE: If we're to tell others, Matt, we need words.

TALBOT: When they came into that room an' found St. Catherine in a corner prayin', with a white dove on her head, did any of them need words then?

PRIEST FIGURE: [*Cry*] What's the book you are reading there, Matt?

TALBOT: 'Tis about the sickness of the mind. Though the poor men that writ it never knew the Gawd that made him. He has the notion that the holy men of the desert, St. Anthony an' d'other lads, were all lunatics.

PRIEST FIGURE: Hm. Pay no heed to it, Matt.

TALBOT: Oh, 'tis heed I pay to it, awright. [*Pause*] Sure the man is right but in a way unbeknownst to him.

PRIEST FIGURE: [*Shocked*] What do you mean?

TALBOT: [*Testy*] I mane what I say! [*Pause*] If to stay in the world 'n do what the world does is to be right in the mind then the saints was all cracked.

Matt Talbot, working-man and mystic, was born in 1856, in the savage poverty of the Dublin slums. He was an early victim of the alcoholism rampant among the poor of the city. At the age of twenty eight he underwent a remarkable change and undertook the pledge of total abstinence from alcohol as part of the Catholic temperance movement. The change, however, had more to do with the secret life which he lived from this point until his death in 1925.

While still remaining an unskilled worker all his life, he followed a daily routine of severe physical penance, fasting and prayer. The full extent of this only became known after his death and a cult of Matt Talbot soon began. . . . The movement towards his canonization as a saint of the Roman Catholic Church began in 1931.

PRIEST FIGURE: It's a peculiar way of puttin' it, Matt.

TALBOT: It's a peculiar world we're in father. What was it St. Anthony saw in the cave? Demons? Not t'all. Demons how are yis! He saw the rest o' the world dressed up for a circus. Ay. All the helter-skelter for what it was. Bastes roarin' 'n screechin' 'n rushin' to perdition! There was no demon only man. 'N after twenty years in the cave 'n he climbed out onta the mountain it must have been a terrible relief for the poor fella. Standin' lookin' across at the Red Sea in the distance. Like a big cloud on the ground, it says in the book. God knows in his wisdom I'm no Anthony. But I do often have the same feelin' comin' outta this room, outta the house in the mornin'. No wan on the streets but the poor misfortunates that haven't slept. I do often see a light like the beginnin' of the world. But then the auld traffic starts 'n I begin to hurry along, ya know first a sorta hard walk, y'know 'n before ya know it I'm in a trot, lathered in sweat, like, runnin'. Ay. [*Slow, sardonic laugh*] Runnin' like a lunatic. [*Pause*] D'ya ever tink, father, there's any foundation in the notion we might be goin' through hell on earth? I do often think so!

PRIEST FIGURE: [*Sententious*] There's a stage when even the holiest of men have doubts. I don't have to tell you. St. John of the Cross. Dark night of the soul and so on.

TALBOT: Stoppit, father—I've me dark night of the soul when I tries to wash me face in de mornings. Dark night is right! Isn't every other night dark?

PRIEST FIGURE: I'm surprised at you, Matt. It's not seemly. Certainly not. The Church—the Church—

TALBOT: I know the Church is God's house!

PRIEST FIGURE: We're not talking about a building, Matt, but a body of knowledge, teaching—faith.

TALBOT: [*Pause*] I believe, father, I believe.

PRIEST FIGURE: I'm your friend, Matt. Your friend.

TALBOT: Oh, ay, ay.

PRIEST FIGURE: But this is ridiculous! Someone like you. For years I marvelled at your faith, your devotion. Come on, Matt! Look. In years

---

Talbot lived through the crucial period of modern Irish history, the last decades of the nineteenth century, the Great Lock Out of Dublin workers in 1913, the rebellion of 1916 and the Independence of the new state.

I wanted to write a play about the mystic and the essentially irreducible division between such extreme individualism and the claims of relationship, of community, society. . . . What I think I wrote was a play about aloneness, its cost to the person and the kind of courage required to sustain it. . . .

from the author's program notes

to come, people will look to your good example, yes, see you as someone to follow in their efforts to—

TALBOT: [*Change*] Don't be sayin' that!

PRIEST FIGURE: Matt—

TALBOT: Don't be sayin' that! [*Anguished tearing at his shirt*] Is it this-this-this yer talkin' about? The coupla chains round me body. Is that it? What does that make me, anyway? It manes nothin' to anyone. How could it when tis only the way for me to know the darkness of me own body. Oders are different. D'yis tink Gawd wants every-wan goin' round with chains?

PRIEST FIGURE: Of course not—I—I

TALBOT: Would anywan need another to copy if they were able to make themselves inta what de be? If y'll excuse me, father, I've no time for the Church devotions when 'tis only people runnin' from them-selves.

PRIEST FIGURE: I can't allow you to talk like that, Matt, about the faith of good people so I can't. No, no.

TALBOT: I knows the people an' I knows the streets. It's a distraction from misery most peoples want in a church, small blame to them.

PRIEST FIGURE: But what about your own devotion to—to St. Teresa and St. Catherine—

TALBOT: Ay, ay. They're a grand coupla girls so they are.

PRIEST FIGURE: [*Uncertainly*] Hm. Yes—yes.

TALBOT: Ya have to stand alone foreninst yer maker. Everywan has to do this hisself. After that there's no company in this life from saint nor sinner.

PRIEST FIGURE: But that's pride, man!

TALBOT: [*Innocently*] I do often pray against pride, father.

PRIEST FIGURE: [*Long pause*] What do you see, Matt?

TALBOT: What do I see?

PRIEST FIGURE: Yes.

TALBOT: I dunno what ya mane, father.

PRIEST FIGURE: Well, I never asked you this before, Matt. I respect the pri-vacy of the soul, I do, I do. But—well, when you pray—when you kneel for hours with arms outstretched, Matt, you must see—you must gain the presence—

TALBOT: [*Brusquely*] Nuthin'.

PRIEST FIGURE: Nothing!

TALBOT: Nuthin'! Nuthin'! Nuthin'!

PRIEST FIGURE: You mean—you mean you—remove yourself?

TALBOT: Oh, I'm there right enough. [*Aggrieved*] Why d'ya ask me? I can't say.

PRIEST FIGURE: I understand, Matt, I understand. You simply place before you some picture of the throne of God, some figures of the heavenly host, some—

TALBOT: Arragh, father, stoppit! [*Pause*] Maybe in the beginning I seen them all, up in the clouds but sure that's only like pictures in the prayer book. 'Twas the dream o' the child in me. Or maybe that's the only way ya can think about them things or talk about them. [*Annoyance*] Sure Gawd Almighty isn't puttin' on a show in the picture palace!

PRIEST FIGURE: [*Lost. Sermonizingly*] We place before us in our mind's eye an image of holy worship. We concentrate ourselves upon it, removing ourselves from the world about us. In this way we come to—

TALBOT: [*Sudden outburst. Very high singsong intonation*] Gawd is wan! In the world everything's more than wan. We die to become wan agin an' there be no numbers to count beyond the grave. There be nuthin' to see when Gawd comes cause there's nothin' oder than yerself cause yerself is wan with what ya see so ya see nuthin' cause ya can only see what's separate than yerself ya can only count whas different, not the same, not the wan, the only— [*Talbot slumps, exhausted. Priest Figure comes right up behind him.*]

PRIEST FIGURE: Matt! Matt!

TALBOT: Whasit?

PRIEST FIGURE: Matt!

TALBOT: Ay. Ay.

PRIEST FIGURE: What is it you wanted, Matt?

TALBOT: [*Shakes his head a few times. Face lights up at memory*] To tell yus de truth, I never wanted anything but to work wid timber—

PRIEST FIGURE: Timber?

TALBOT: Ay. Timber. I used to walk round an' round the sheds when the fresh lumber used to come off the boats. Piles 'n piles to the roof. 'N I'd run me hand along the grain. 'N I'd fill me smell with the sap. Long ways away they came from where there's big woods. 'N I'd see the trees cause timber never dies when 'tis cut, only changin' with age.

PRIEST FIGURE: [*Slowly in a whisper*] And what do you want of me, Matt Talbot.

TALBOT: An' who are you?

[*Behind him Priest Figure disrobes to an old woman, long dress, long grey hair. She places her hands on Talbot's shoulders, gently rocking him from side to side. Talbot closes his eyes and rocks silently for a little while.*]

TALBOT: Oh, Mother! Mother! Mother! Oh, Mother of God!

. . .

TALBOT: Get thee behind me, Satan! For thou sacoures not the things that be of God, but the things that be of MEN. Leave me be! There's a little distance left to me to go. Leave me to go alone!

[*The other figures slink away and exit from the set. Weakly, he kneels, blesses himself*]

TALBOT: [*In prayer*] A very little while and all will be over with thee here. See how it stands with thee in the next life. Man today is, and tomorrow he is seen no more. An' when he is taken away from sight, he is quickly also out of mind. [*He stands, rooting about*] Hafta go to Mass. Hafta move quick. Where's me hat gone to? [*Finds hat, jacket, muffler, staggers out to side of stage. His movements compared to the earlier part of play, are pathetic, weak. As the church bell rings, he sets off to opposite side of stage, kneels. Another church bell, he starts back. Reaches centre stage, falters, falls to his knees, breathless. Takes off his hat, holds it to his breast. His tone is half story-telling, with an innocent awe at his story. Priest Figure as old woman comes and kneels behind him*] D'old man worked at the bench, shavin' the yella timbers in the sunlight. An' the boy used to help him. They worked together. They never spoke. They never needed a word. Nuthin' was heard but the sound of timber. Then wan day—wan day, the boy left. Again, nare a word. He put down the tools outta his hands. D'old man came to the door wid him. They kissed wan anoder. Den the moder came like a shadda from the house an' she kissed the boy, too. Then the boy walked down the road in the dust 'n the hot sun. 'N way in the far distance of the city he could hear them, the hammers batin' the timber into the shape of the cross.

[*He puts his hat down, bends as if to lie down to rest and slowly collapses. He forms a pietà tableau with Old Woman. The front of the great box swings closed. First Man, Second Man and Woman may be seen in outline looking into the closed box which is ablaze with light*]

JOHN McGAHERN

Along the Edges

EVENING

'I must go now.' She tried to rise from the bed.

'Stay.' His arms about her pale shoulders held her back as she pressed upwards with her hands. 'Let me kiss you there once more.'

'Don't be silly,' she laughed and fell back into his arms. 'I have to go.' Her body trembled with low laughter as he went beneath the sheet to kiss her; and then they stretched full length against one another, kissing over and back on the mouth, in a last grasping embrace.

'I wish I could eat and drink you.'

'Then I'd be gone,' she pushed him loose with her palms. They both rose and dressed quickly.

'I'll leave you home. It's too late for you to go alone.' Lately she had seemed to want to assert their separateness after each lovemaking, when she should be the more his.

'All right, but I don't mind,' she said, a seeming challenge in her eyes.

'Besides I want to,' he leaned to kiss her on the side of the throat as she drew on her jacket. They stole down the stairs, and outside he held the door firmly until the catch clicked quietly behind them. The fading moonlight was weak on the leaves of the single laurel in the front garden, and he grew uneasy at the apparent reluctance with which she seemed to give him her gloved hand on the pavement, with the way she hurried, their separate footsteps loud in the silence of the sleeping suburbs.

They'd met just after broken love affairs, and had drifted casually into going out together two or three evenings every week. They went to cinemas or dancehalls or restaurants, to the races at Leopardstown or the Park, making no demands on one another, sharing only one another's pleasures, making love together as on this night in his student's room.

Sensing her hard separateness in their separate footsteps as they walked towards her home in the sleeping suburbs, he began to feel that by now

103

there should be more between them than this sensual ease. Till now, for him, the luxury of this ease had been perfect. This uncomplicated pleasure seemed the very fullness of life, seemed all that life could yearn towards, and yet it could not go on forever. There comes a point in all living things when they must change or die, and maybe they had passed that point already without noticing, and that already he had lost her, when he was longing to draw closer.

'When will we meet again?' he asked her as usual at the gate before she went in.

'When do you want?' she asked as usual.

'Saturday, at eight, outside the Metropole.'

'Saturday—at eight, then,' she agreed.

There was no need to seek for more. His anxiety had been groundless. Wednesdays and Saturdays were always given. No matter how hard the week was he had always Saturdays and Wednesdays to look forward to: he could lean upon their sensual ease and luxury as reliably as upon a drug. Now that Saturday was once more promised his life was perfectly arranged. With all the casualness of the self-satisfied male, he kissed her good-night and it caused her to look sharply at him before she went in, but he noticed nothing. He waited until he heard the latch click and then went whistling home through the empty silent streets just beginning to grow light.

That next Saturday he stayed alone in the room, studying by the light of a bulb fixed on a chianti bottle, the texts and diagrams spread out on newspaper that shielded his arms from the cold of the marble top that had once been a washstand, the faded velvet curtain drawn on the garden and hot day outside, on cries of the ice-cream wagons, on the long queues within the city for buses to the sea, on the sea of Dollymount and the swimmers going in off the rocks, pleasures sharpened a hundredfold by the drawn curtain. Finally, late in the afternoon, when he discovered that he had just reached the bottom of a page without taking in a single sentence, he left the room and went down to the front. At the corner shop he bought an orange and sat on a bench. The sea lay dazzling in the heat out past the Bull and Howth Head. An old couple and a terrier with a newspaper in his mouth went past him as he peeled the orange. Music came from a transistor somewhere. Exams should be held in winter, he thought tiredly, for he seemed to be looking at the people walking past him and lolling on other benches or on the thin grass, on the shimmering sea itself, and the dark buildings across the bay, as if through plate glass.

Still, at eight o'clock she would come to him, out of the milling crowds about the Metropole, her long limbs burning nakedly beneath the swinging folds of the brown dress that hid them and flaunted them, the face that came towards him and then drew back as she laughed, and he would begin to live again. He had all that forgetting to go towards, the losing of the day in all the sweetness of her night. He rose, threw the orange peel into a wire basket, and walked back to the room. He imagined he must have been working for about an hour when he heard the heavy knocker of the front door go; but when he looked at his watch he found that he had been working already for more than two hours, which must be the greater part of happiness.

After the knocking, he listened as the door was opened, and heard voices—the landlord's, probably the vegetable man or the coal man—but went quite still as steps came up the stairs towards the door of the room, the landlord's steps because of the heavy breathing. A knock came on the door, and the fat, little old landlord put his head in, stains of egg yolk on his lapels. 'A visitor for you,' he whispered and winked.

She stood below in the hallway beside the dark bentwood coat rack, her legs crossed as if for a casual photo, arms folded, a tense smile fixed on her face, her hair brushed high. She had never come to the house on her own before. Was something wrong? Or had she grown impatient waiting to meet him at the Metropole and come to him early?

'Thanks,' she said to the landlord when he came down.

'Won't you come up?' he called from the head of the stairs.

The landlord made a face and winked again as she climbed.

'I'm sorry coming like this,' she said.

'No, that doesn't matter,' he said as he closed the door. 'I was just about to get ready to go to meet you. This way we can have even more time together.'

'It's not that,' she said quickly. 'I came round to see if you'd mind putting the evening off.'

'Why, is there something wrong?'

'No. It's just that Margaret has come up of a sudden from the country.'

'That's your friend from school days?'

'Yes. She hardly ever comes up. And I thought you wouldn't mind giving the evening up so that we could go out together.'

'Did she not tell you she was coming up?' The whole long-looked-forward-to balm of the evening was threatened by this whim or accident.

'No. She came on a chance. Someone was coming up and offered her a lift.'

'And she expects you to drop everything and dance attendance on her?'

'She doesn't expect anything,' she met his annoyance with her own.

'All I can say is that it's very poor. You must have cared very little about the evening if you can change it that quickly.'

'Well, if you're that huffed about it we can go through with the evening. I didn't think you'd mind.'

'Where is this Margaret?'

'She's outside. Why do you want to know?'

'I suppose I should pay my respects and let the pair of you away.'

'Don't put yourself out.'

'It'll be a pleasure,' but then his anger broke before he opened the door. 'If that's all our going out means to you we might as well forget the whole thing.'

'What do you mean?' she asked.

'We might as well break the whole thing off,' he said less certainly.

'That can be easily arranged.'

'It might be arranged for you.' The door was open and they both came downstairs in silent anger.

Outside, Margaret was leaning against the railing by the bus stop. She was a large country girl, with a mane of black hair and broad athlete's shoulders. The three made polite awkward conversation that did not cover over the tenseness till the bus came.

'I hope you have a nice evening,' he said as they boarded the bus.

'That's what we intend,' her lovely face was unflinching, but Margaret waved. He watched them take a seat together on the lower deck and waited to see if they would look back, but they did not.

Rattling coins, he went towards the telephone box at the end of the road to ring round to see if any of his friends were free for the evening.

They did not meet again till two Saturdays later, at the Metropole, as usual at eight. She had on a floppy blue hat and dark glasses. Her summer dress was sleeveless, and she had a race card in her long gloved hands.

'You must have just come from the races.'

'I was at the Park. I even won some money,' she smiled her old roguish smile.

'You must be hungry then. Why don't we go somewhere nice to eat?'

'That's fine with me,' she said with all her mocking brightness. 'I can take you—this evening—with the winnings.'

'If that suits you. I have money too.'

'You took long enough in calling,' she said with a flash of real resentment.

'It didn't seem that it'd make much difference to you. It'd be nice for me to think I was wrong, but that's how it seemed when I thought it out.'

'Where are we going?' she stopped, and that they were adversaries now was in the open.

'To Bernardo's. We always had good times there. Even coming from the races you look very beautiful,' he said by way of appeasement.

The resturant was just beginning to fill. The blindman was playing the piano at its end, his white stick leaning against the dark varnish. They ate in tenseness and mostly silence, the piano thumping indifferently away.

She had never looked so beautiful; it was like an old tune, now that he was about to lose her. It was as if this evening was an echo of a darker evening and was uniting with it to try to break him.

'You're not eating much,' she said when she saw him struggle with the veal.

'It must be the damned exam,' he said. 'It's starting next week. And, after all, I wasn't at the races.'

'That's true,' she laughed.

'I'm sorry about that ridiculous fuss I made a few weeks back,' he said openly.

'It's all right. It's all over now.'

'Do you think you'll be able to come back with me this evening?' For a wild sensual moment he hoped everything would suddenly be as it had been before.

'Is it for—the usual?' she asked slowly.

'I suppose.'

'No,' she shook her head, and it sounded like a more gentle toll of another No.

'Why?'

'I don't see any point. Do you?'

'We've often . . . many times before.'

'We've gone on that way for too long,' she said.

'But I love you. And I thought—when things are more settled—we might be married.'

'No,' she was looking at him with affection and trying to speak softly and slowly. 'You must know that the only time things are settled, if they are ever settled, is *now*. And I've had some hard thinking to do since that last evening. You were quite right to be angry. If I was seriously interested in you I'd not have broken the date for someone coming casually to town. There was a time I thought I was getting involved with you, but then you didn't seem interested, and women are practical. I'm very fond of you, and we've had good times, and maybe the good times just went on for too long, when we just should have had a romp, and let it go,' she spoke as if it already belonged to a life that was over.

'Is there no hope, no hope at all, that it might change?' he asked with nothing more than an echo of desperation.

Through the sensual caresses, laughter, evenings of pleasure, the instinct had been beginning to assemble a dream, a hope; soon, little by little, without knowing, he would have woken to find that he had fallen in love. We assemble a love as we assemble our life and grow so absorbed in the assembling that we wake in terror at the knowledge that all that we have built is terminal, that in our pain we must undo it again.

There had been that moment too that might have been grasped at the flood, and had not, and love had died—she had admitted as much. It would have led on to what? To happiness, for a while, or the absence of this present sense of loss, or to some other sense of loss. . . .

He thought he saw that moment, as well that moment now as any other: an evening in O'Connell Street, a Saturday evening like any other, full of the excitement of the herding. She had taken his arm.

'My young sister is to be engaged tomorrow. Why don't we drive up? There's to be a party. And afterwards we could have the weekend on our own,' and when he answered, 'It's the one weekend I can't,' and started to explain, he saw the sudden glow go from her face; an impoverishment of calculation replaced it that had made him momentarily afraid. Anyhow, it was all evening now. That crossroad at which they had actually separated had been passed long before in the day.

'No,' she said gently. 'And you'd not be so reckless if I'd said Yes. We were both more in love with the idea of falling in love, of escaping.'

'Still it's no fun walking round the world on your own.'

'It's not so bad as being with someone you can't stand after the pleasure has worn off,' she said as if she were looking past the evening.

'I give up,' he said and called for the bill.

'Ring me sometime,' she said as she got on the bus outside.

'Right, then,' he waved and knew neither of them would. They had played at a game of life, and had not fallen, and were now as indifferent to one another, outside the memory of pleasure, as if they were both already dead to one another. If they were not together in the evening how could they ever have been so in the morning. . . .

And if she had come to him instead of leaving him, those limbs would never reach whomever they were going to. . . .

And why should we wish the darkness harm, it is our element; or curse the darkness because we are doomed to love in it, and die. . . .

And those that move along the edges can see it so until they fall.

MORNING

'What does your friend do for a living?' the man asked the blonde woman in front of him after Marion, an enormous ungainly girl, had gone to the Ladies in Bernardo's.

'She's not a friend. In fact, she's more than a friend. She's a client. She's a star. A pop star.' The woman smiled as she drew slowly on her cigarette. 'You're behind the times. You see, I'm here to bring you up to date.'

'But how can she be a pop star?'

'You mean because she's ugly? That doesn't matter. That helps. The public's tired of long, pale beautiful slenders. Ugliness and energy—

that's what's wanted now. And she has a good voice. She can belt them out.'

'Does she have men friends and all that?'

'As many as she wants. Proposals. Everything a woman's supposed to want.'

'She's certainly not what you'd call beautiful.'

'Publicity makes her beautiful. It moves her closer to the sun. In fact, it is the sun and still has its worshippers.'

'It doesn't make her beautiful to me,' the man said doggedly, 'though I think you're beautiful.'

'What *is* beauty? A good clothes rack or a good flesh rack? I don't know.'

'Whatever it is, you have it.' He changed, 'It doesn't look as if Peter will come back now.'

'No,' she said. 'Peter isn't trustworthy. I wish they'd let the blindman go home,' she said as he struck up another number on the piano.

'I suppose, for them, it's the hopeful hours,' the man referred to the large noisy table in the centre of the restaurant. They had come from a party, and had bribed the blindman to play on after he had risen about midnight to catch his usual garage bus to Inchicore.

'Do you have anything to do with Peter?'

'How?' she asked sharply.

'Sleep with him?'

She laughed. 'I've never even thought of Peter that way. He's a contact. In the trade,' and without warning she leaned across the table and placed the burning tip of the cigarette against the back of the man's hand.

'What did you want to do that for?' he asked angrily.

'I felt like it. I suppose I should be sorry.'

'No,' he changed. 'Not if you come home with me.'

'To sleep with you?' she parodied.

'That would be best of all but it's not important. We can spend the morning together,' he said eagerly.

'All right,' she nodded.

They were both uneasy after the agreement. They had left one level and had not entered any other.

'Do you think I should go to see if anything's the matter with Marion?'

'Maybe. Wait a little,' he said.

Marion was pale when she came back. 'I'm afraid I'm not used to the wine,' she apologized.

'I'm sorry, but we can go now. Do you think you will be all right?'

'I'll be fine,' she said.

'Anyhow, you'll both see Peter tomorrow. He said he'd definitely be at the reception.'

The last thing their eyes rested on before they went through the door the Italian manager was holding open was the blindman's cane leaning against the side of the piano.

'Do you think they'll make the poor man play all night?' she asked.

'He seems satisfied. I even heard them arranging for a taxi to take him home. I suppose we too should be thinking of a taxi.'

'I'd rather walk, if that's all right.'

They walked slowly towards the hotel. The night was fine but without moon or stars. Just before they got to the hotel, the man shook hands with Marion, and the two women walked together to the hotel door. They stood a while in conversation there before the star went in and the blonde woman turned back towards the man.

'It always makes me uncomfortable. Being part of the couple, leaving the single person alone,' he said.

'The single person is usually glad to be left alone.'

'I know that but it doesn't stop the feeling,' it was the same feeling one got passing hushed hospitals late at night.

'Anyhow, you've had your wish. We're together,' the woman said, and they kissed for the first time. They crossed to the taxi rank facing the railings of the Green, and they did not speak in the taxi. What hung between them might be brutal and powerful, but it was as frail as the flesh out of which it grew, for any endurance. They had chosen one another because of the empty night, and the wrong words might betray them early, making one hateful to the other; but even the right words, if there were right words, had not the power to force it. It had to grow or wither like a wild flower. What they needed most was patience, luck, and that twice-difficult thing, to be lucky in one another, and at the same time, and to be able to wait for that time.

'Will I switch on the light?' he asked her as he let her into the flat.

'Whatever you like.'

'Then I'd rather not.'

After they had kissed he said, 'There's my room and the spare room. I don't mind if you think it too soon and use the spare room.'

'Wait,' she said softly, and her arms leaned heavily round his shoulders, as if she had forgotten him, and was going over her life to see if she could gather it into this one place. Suddenly she felt him trembling. She pulled him towards her.

'Do you bring many people back like this?' she asked close to morning, almost proprietorially.

'No. Not for ages.'

'Why?'

'First you have to find a person who'll consent,' he half joked. 'And there's not much use after a while unless there seems a chance of something more.'

'Of what?'

'Of it going on, I suppose.'

There was a silence in which a moth blundering about the half-darkness overhead was too audible.

'And you, have you men?' he asked awkwardly.

'No. Until recently I had one man.'

'What happened?'

'Nothing. He was married. It sounds like a record.'

'It's all a record, but it seems the only record worth hearing.'

And it only takes one person to make it new again, he thought, the quality of the making being all that mattered.

'Well, the poor quality record went this way. The man in question had a quite awful dilemma, and he suffered, how he suffered, especially with me. You see, he was torn between his wife and myself, and he could not make up his mind. Women are, I think, more primal than men. They don't bother too much about who pays the bill as long as they get what they want. So I gave him an ultimatum. And when he still couldn't make up his mind I left him. That must sound pretty poor stuff.'

'No. It sounds true.'

That hard as porcelain singleness of women, seeming sometimes to take pleasure in cruelty, was part of their beauty too.

'Would you like to be married?'

'Yes. And you?'

'I suppose I would.'

'You know that speech about those that are married or kind to their friends. They become olives, pomegranate, mulberry, flowers, precious stones, eminent stars.'

'I'd rather stay as I am,' she laughed.

'But you still see yourself at it.'

'That's just self-consciousness.'

'And pain isn't pain. It's just morbid organs monitoring distress. It's all wrong.'

'Well, let it be wrong then. It's all we have and that just happens to be the way we have it. We didn't choose it. Any more than those before us, or those that may come after us.'

When they rose and washed in the flat in all its daylight, it seemed as if it was not only a new day but the beginning of a new life. The pictures, the plates, the table in its stolidity seemed to have been set askew by the accidental night, to want new shapes, to look comical in their old places. The books on the wall, the hours spent with them, seemed to have belonged to an old relative to whom one did not even owe a responsibility of affection. Gaily one could pick or discard among them, choosing only those useful to the new. For, like a plant, the old outer leaves would have to lie withered for new green shoots to push upwards at the heart.

'What are you thinking?'

'Nothing much. Of another morning. A Paris morning, opening shutters, a water truck was going past, and behind came four Algerians with long-handled brooms.'

'Were you alone or with someone?' he was ashamed of the first pang of irrational jealousy, and it was as if some old record that should be drowned out was starting up again in spite of everything.

'Actually, I was alone. I suppose one is mostly alone in those mornings,' her gravity as much as a small child's took all the light to itself.

They had come from four separate people, two men and two women, lying together in two separate nights; and those two nights were joined in the night they had left, had grown into the morning.

She was not garlanded by farms or orchards, by any house by the sea, by neither judges nor philosophers. She stood as she was, belonging to the morning, as they both hoped to belong to the evening. They could not possess the morning, no more than they could disagree with it or go against its joy.

She was wearing what she wore at the dinner while the blindman played, a dress of blue denim, buttoned down the front, and on her stockingless feet were thonged sandals.

'What are you going to do today?'

'I have to go to the hotel, and then to the reception. I suppose we'll see the busy Peter there. After that I'm free. And you?'

'I'm free all day.'

'Maybe we'll begin to learn a little more about one another then.'

'As long as we know it'll be more of nothing. We know hardly anything now and we may never be as well off.' They would have to know that they could know nothing to go through the low door of love, the door that was the same doorway between the self and the other everywhere.

'Well, anyhow we have to face the day,' she said, dispelling it in one movement; and they took one another's hands as they went to meet the day, the day already following them, and all about them.

THOMAS MURPHY

from *A Crucial Week in the Life of a Grocer's Assistant*

SCENE TWO

[*Mr. Brown's grocery shop. About 11:00 a.m. Mr. Brown is looking out at the quiet street off. He is about sixty. John Joe, wearing a shop coat stands behind the counter. They are sipping tea. Pause.*]

MR. BROWN [*To himself*]: Quiet . . . But they're not in the co-op up the road either. People round here like the personal touch, the chat across the counter . . . They are not up in the co-op either, sir.

[*Footsteps off approaching. Mr. Brown waits expectantly. The footsteps pass the shop and fade.*]

MR. BROWN: Mrs. Quigley.

JOHN JOE [*Suddenly*]: But it's a nice morning though, Mr. Brown.

MR. BROWN: If Horan's van comes this evening and I'm not here, only take the one side of bacon off him this week. There's no demand for it. [*Sighs*]. The money isn't circulating. [*Angry for a moment.*] The driver of that van is an awful harum-scarum. [*Pause.*] The money is not circulating, sir.

[*Pause. Mr. Brown finishes his tea. He starts to move away; stops, thinks; then:*]

MR. BROWN: Was that Lipton's tea?

JOHN JOE: 'Twas.

[*Mr. Brown nods gravely and exits to rear of shop. Pause. Footsteps approaching. Pakey Garvey enters. Pakey is home from England for his father's funeral. He is four or five years younger than John Joe. His humour*]

*is bitter and cynical. He wears a three-quarter length mackintosh with ep-
aulets. On his sleeve a black diamond to symbolize he is in mourning.
John Joe does not recognize him for a moment. Then he greets him eagerly.*]

JOHN JOE: Aw, jay, how yeh, Pakey! [*Then he remembers Pakey is in
    mourning; suddenly solemn-faced.*]

[*Pakey grimaces cynically and sighs in an exaggerated way—and quite
openly—at John Joe's change of expression. He knows the rigmarole of
sympathies that are coming. He plays along. He flicks his hand out of his
pocket for the hand-shake.*]

PAKEY: How yeh, sonny!
JOHN JOE [*Unsure*]: I—I was sorry to hear about your father, Pake.
PAKEY [*Sniffs*]: I know that; everyone was sorry.
JOHN JOE: That's—that's the way.
PAKEY: That's the way, sonny.

[*Short pause.*]

PAKEY: } I came in to—
JOHN JOE: } He lived—
PAKEY: What?
JOHN JOE: He had a good long—longish—life.
PAKEY: Oh, he had. Fifty-two, John Joe.
JOHN JOE: Jay, that's a lovely coat you have on, Pake.
PAKEY: What?
JOHN JOE: When are you going back to London, Pake?
PAKEY: Tomorrow morning. I've enough of the knockers and the craw-
    thumpers after four days in this place. Is "His Holiness" in?
JOHN JOE: He's just gone out to the johns for a minute. [*Laughs.*] Eleven
    o'clock is his time.
PAKEY: Yes. I was looking at that messenger bike out there on my way in.
    Many's the trip I done on it for him. Remember? Seventeen-and-six
    a week he was paying me. But he used to give me time off for going
    up to the church for confession and that. "Pray for the Russians,
    Patrick."
JOHN JOE: Ary, he's all right.
PAKEY: If I was home in time my brother would not have ordered the cof-
    fin here.
JOHN JOE: How do you like London?
PAKEY: What?

JOHN JOE: Piccadilly, hah? Cricklewood for the crack. Tottenham Court Road. Camden Town for the good lie down, and Hammersmith for dancing. Don't they have lovely names on places?

PAKEY: Were you ever—?

JOHN JOE: No, but, you know. I meet fellahs like yourself, like, now and again, home on holidays.

PAKEY (*Takes out a fat wallet*): Ah, sure, you have a good job here. [*He hands John Joe two pay-packets.*]

JOHN JOE: What? £41-7-4! A week?

PAKEY: They used call me "Bags" around here.

JOHN JOE: And what are you doing over there to be—

PAKEY: And they used call my father—

JOHN JOE [*Reading second pay-packet*]: £43-11-2—

PAKEY: "Rags."

JOHN JOE: That's great money, Pake.

PAKEY: "Rags" . . . But isn't it a wonder you never—

JOHN JOE: I never had any wish to leave.

PAKEY: I thought that must be it.

JOHN JOE [*Phoney laugh*]: Is it company you want over there?

PAKEY: Yeh?

JOHN JOE: No-no, I'll tell you. A few years ago, a few of us in Dublin one weekend, and I had half-a-mind to take the boat and—[*He makes obscene "V" gesture*]—the lot.

PAKEY: Yeh?

JOHN JOE: I nearly did.

PAKEY: Yeh?

JOHN JOE: I nearly—I—[*Pakey takes back his pay-packets.*] But—but— but, tell me, tell me this, Pake, apart from the money over there—

PAKEY: Apart from *what*?

JOHN JOE: What I mean is . . .

PAKEY: Yeh? . . . I'm surprised at anyone born and reared in this holy town to make a statement like that. Ah, but they love the dead around here.

[*Mr. Brown enters, hurrying to Pakey, gushing, hand outstretched.*]

MR. BROWN: Patrick! Patrick!

PAKEY: Malachy! Malachy! [*Deftly flicks out his hand again for hand-shake.*] I came in to settle up with you for the coffin.

MR. BROWN: Well now, Patrick, you know I'm not worried about the bill. You know that now, don't you, Patrick?

PAKEY: Yes—yes, I know that well, Malachy, *But.*

MR. BROWN: Nor was I ever worried in dealings with the Garveys.

PAKEY: Except the time—

MR. BROWN: In dealings with the Garveys, sir.

PAKEY [*Groans aloud, rolling his eyes up at the ceiling.*]: But—if—we—could, Mr. Brown get down to—

MR. BROWN: But wasn't it the sad journey you had to make?

PAKEY: 'Twas.

MR. BROWN: 'Twas.

PAKEY: 'Twas.

MR. BROWN: 'Twas. 'Twas indeed.

PAKEY: 'Twas. 'Twas, John Joe?

JOHN JOE [*Trying to restrain his laughter.*]: 'Twas.

MR. BROWN: It was, sir. [*Mr. Brown realizes the mockery, but this is the only way he can play it.*] But he had a good life.

PAKEY: He had, half-starved. Fond of the bottle, too, Mr. Brown?

MR. BROWN: He was, he w—Aw! No now, Patrick. Ah-haa, you were always the joker, always the—

PAKEY: Not a great sodality man, Mr. Brown?

MR. BROWN: Always the joker.

PAKEY: But maybe he was ashamed of his suit.

MR. BROWN: Well, you never changed. [*Solemn again.*] No, Patrick, your father, Bartley Garvey, could take a drink, and he could carry it. And that was no flaw in Bartley Garvey's character.

PAKEY [*Solemnly*]: Musha, poor auld fuckin' "Rags."

MR. BROWN: Ah—well—yes. But you're doing well?

PAKEY: Oh, yes, Mr. Brown.

MR. BROWN: Saving your money, Patrick?

PAKEY: Oh yes. And when I have enough saved—

MR. BROWN: You'll come home.

PAKEY: I will.

MR. BROWN: And you'll be welcome.

PAKEY: And I'll buy out this town, Mr. Brown.

MR. BROWN: You will, sir.

PAKEY: And then I'll burn it to the ground.

MR. BROWN: Hah-haa, hah-haa, joker, joker! Well now, Patrick, we're all pleased you like England and getting on well, but I'm sure you're in a hurry now, and—

PAKEY: Sure, it's a lovely country, England. And the bosses all pay great wages and—

MR. BROWN: That's good—they do—that's—

PAKEY: No old hypocrites over there at all—

MR. BROWN: I heard that.

PAKEY: Sure, it's a great country. Great pagan people, the English.

MR. BROWN: Very nice people, we're told.

PAKEY: They mind their own business. And they don't call a man—a fool —if he's trying to enjoy himself in life.

MR. BROWN: Well—well now, not many young fellahs could afford the burial you gave him. And you're well able to support your mother now. We won't be delaying you, Patrick: I'm sure you have things to do. I'll just get the bill from the office. No one can say you didn't put a decent coffin on him.

[*Mr. Brown exits to office.*]

PAKEY: I was afraid they might be talking all right.

JOHN JOE: But is it that good over there?

PAKEY: Money! To save, spend, send home, be independent, see them as they are, or whatever you want to do with it.

JOHN JOE: But—

PAKEY: But, first step, you mustn't be afraid to say—[*He makes obscene "V" gesture*]—to this place.

JOHN JOE: Oh, there's more to it than just that.

PAKEY: Well, if there is, it's too much for you. [*Calls as he marches into the office*] You didn't drop dead in there yourself, did you, Mr. Brown?

[*Pakey exits, marching into the office.*]

MR. BROWN [*Off*]: Oh, come in, come in, Patrick. I'm just totting up . . .

JOHN JOE: Well, if it's that good, what are you so bitter about?

[*John Joe takes a new packet of cigarettes from under the counter, open them, lights one and pockets the remainder. All the time looking in the direction Pakey has taken. Then he collects up the dirty cups and exits with them to rear of shop. Pakey and Mr. Brown enter. Mr. Brown showing Pakey out.*]

MR. BROWN: Do you remember when you used caddy for me out in the golf-links? The short little trousers on you. Did I treat you fair? Did I or didn't I always give you a tanner more than Simon Manton?

PAKEY: Like any sportsman, you liked to find your ball in a good lie always, Mr. Brown.

MR. BROWN: . . . Well, you're off in the morning then?

PAKEY: Were you ever in England, Mr. Brown?

MR. BROWN: Oh, I was. Well, it was just to touch down at London airport one time, for something or other, on our way to Lourdes.

PAKEY: Ah yes. And your piles were never cured. Look at that now! And they say faith can move mountains.

[*Pakey exits. Mr. Brown's smile starts to fade.*]

SCENE NINE — SATURDAY

[*The hay shed. It is nearing dawn. John Joe and Mona are sitting on the hay. Pause.*]

MONA: I was glad you showed up tonight . . . You didn't tell me where you were for the past few nights. It seemed like . . . ages . . . Do you know? You *are* a very bad court . . . John Joe.

JOHN JOE: Yes.

MONA: Did you think any more about going away?

JOHN JOE: No.

MONA: Are you feeling sorry for yourself or something?

JOHN JOE: What?

[*Pause*]

MONA: Oh, do you know what Jimmy said to me once? Out in front of Daddy and all. We were sitting down to Sunday lunch and Jimmy was only eleven then. But he said, "Mona," he said, "I notice you have very good childbearing hips." I was mortified. I was only a second-year at school and it was during the holidays, and—

JOHN JOE: School for young ladies with fat bullocks. Bullocks, I said, mind. Their daddiadies' bullocks at a hundred pounds apiece. What about me and Agnes Smith with thin chickens out in the back yard?

[*Pause*]

MONA: Oh, and my best pal at school—[*She stops short; thinks. Then, almost a new Mona*] I want to talk to you. But how can I, with this— atmosphere—between us? And I have to say something, anything, the first silly old thing that comes into my head, to break it. It's childish. And I'm certainly not a child. I know what I want. And I have no—illusions. You must make up your mind. I know it's not because you're afraid. If it was that I wouldn't be here.

JOHN JOE: Oh? Thanks. That's great.

MONA: We can't keep talking about—

JOHN JOE: No, we can't keep talking about!

MONA: Well, that's all you're doing. I've made my decision.

JOHN JOE: And all I do is talk?

MONA: Yes.

JOHN JOE: Oh?

MONA: Well, do you think it's any easier for me?

JOHN JOE: That dress, can you enjoy it?

MONA: What?

JOHN JOE: I can't enjoy this sportscoat.

MONA: I know, I understand—

JOHN JOE: No. Do you feel guilty for every sip of a drink you take?

MONA: I know what you mean, but—

JOHN JOE: No, it's not that. Do you take a deep breath every time you get outside your own door?—Out of your own street?

MONA: Well, don't start feeling sorry for them.

JOHN JOE: Seeing corny pictures of them, martyrs. See? Do you feel that?

MONA: Are you boasting or complaining?

JOHN JOE: What?

MONA: There's a train out of here on Monday morning.

JOHN JOE: You don't understand.

MONA: I've money.

JOHN JOE: No! Lookity! [*Takes coins out of his pocket.*] I've money! Three whole full shillings and a sprazzy! [*Wanting to hurt her.*] Do you wish you could be poor for me? [*Turns away; to himself:*] It's not the money. [*Turns back to her; cynically*] Aa, you're very nice, Mona. Mona, you're very nice.

MONA: What's wrong with being nice?

JOHN JOE: Aa, you're very—That Mullins! Them Smiths! Them—I'll kick the daylights out of them!

MONA [*Beginning to cry*]: We could hitch.

JOHN JOE: You don't understand at all. Do you feel guilty for every cigarette you smoke? And how can I do anything until I find out what's wrong with that?

MONA: We could leave.

JOHN JOE: It's not just a case of staying or going. It's something to do with Frank, and Pakey, and others like me who left. And others like Miko and Mullins and me who stayed. It's something to do with that. Does that mean anything to you?—What exactly do you think of that?

MONA [*Crying*]: I think you're wonderful.

JOHN JOE [*Stopped for a moment by her sincerity*]: Oh—but—he—has—high—notions—you—know, the gravedigger's son has! Ah yes: maybe that's all that's wrong with him. What are you crying for?

MONA: I'm not crying.

JOHN JOE: Fine—All right—Yes—Okay. [*He tosses away a coin.*]

MONA: You want to get rid of me, don't you?

JOHN JOE: What?

MONA: That would solve half your problem, wouldn't it?

JOHN JOE: Aw God! [*Then with a wild movement he throws away the remaining coins.*] Yes—It would—Right—Fine! I'm tired of it. This romance. We'll finish it! It's ridiculous. And let's hope they'll all be happy now. Come on. We'd better go. . . . Well, come on. It's dawn outside.

MONA: I hope you don't ever do this to any girl again.

JOHN JOE: Aw, for Christ's sake!

MONA: Well, I wouldn't give in.

JOHN JOE: You don't know anything about it!

MONA: I'm willing to take a stand—

JOHN JOE: What do I mean to you? No more than to anybody else. What do I mean to anybody else besides my mother, and what good is that? I've gone through this—"love"—with dozens, hundreds of other girls. I've never felt anything for you. And I don't feel guilty or anything. You were the one who approached me one night. You mean nothing to me. You are a silly, stupid bitch. Whore if you could be. What means anything to you? Mummy, big farm, daddy; the priest plays golf with daddy; the bishop knows daddy; money in the bank. Where does John-Balls-Joe come in? For favours, pity? In a few years' time you'll give a nice little "haw-haw" at all this. In love, Jasus, love! Come on if you're coming.

MONA [*Composed*]: . . . I'll go first. You'd better not be seen walking me home. [*As she exits.*] They might let *me* alone too now.

DESMOND O'GRADY

Prologue

Who saw everything
to the ends of the land,
began at the start
of a primary road.

Who saw the mysteries,
knew secret things,
went a long journey;
found the whole story
cut in stone.

His purpose: praise, search,
his appointed pain,
and the countries of the world
that house his image.

Weary, worn from his labours,
he returned and told
what he'd seen and learned
to help kill the winter.

Village

It would have been, had the toss of the thing fallen differently,
the side of the coin reversed, a simpler scene:
you proud in that magnificent peasant way, rehearsed
in the country's lean

give and take with talk, crossing the square
at evening under the eyes of the young rakes
of lads with their backs to the walls, their day in the fields
        done. From flakes

of one of them's talk, caught by your selfconscious ears,
you'd mark him apart as a stranger come for work
to the district. In a place like this—with form the silence of elders
        sucking a stalk

or a pipe at the corner, and the animal eyes of the young
single men pawing your thighs—so slight an encounter
would hold enough of the long rope of promise to tie
        the knot in love's halter.

Purpose

I looked at my days and saw that
with the first affirmation of summer
I must leave all I knew: the house,
the familiarity of family,
companions and memories of childhood,
a future cut out like a tailored suit,
a settled life among school friends.

I looked face to face at my future:
I saw voyages to distant places,
saw the daily scuffle for survival
in foreign towns with foreign tongues
and small rented rooms on companionless
nights with sometimes the solace
of a gentle anonymous arm on the pillow.

I looked at the faces about me
and saw my days' end as a returned ship,
its witness singing in the rigging.

I saw my life and I walked out to it,
as a seaman walks out alone at night from
his house down to the port with his bundled
belongings, and sails into the dark.

Man and Woman

We began while the year ended.
Two innocents knowing nothing
of the world, we met
in a continental capital—two
foreigners from opposite points
of the compass. I spoke,
with mythological memory, of my
melancholic sea; you
of the desert and inscrutable
ways of the ancient world.

Knowing nobody, we learned
to know each other—as two
travellers will, standing
at a crossroads waiting to continue
on the next leg of their journey.

Your eyes seemed two black stones
at the green sea's edge, polished
by the lap wave's late day's motion;
your limbs, palms in an evening breeze;
your body, opulent as omniscience.

We began while the year ended—
two innocents knowing nothing of the world,
desiring mutual cognisance.

If I Went Away

A Version from the Irish

If I went away I should never come back,
but hike the hills, sound each hollow,
tramp the stony goat-herd track
and my own wild will happily follow.

My heart is as black as a burned door,
or the burnt out coal in a kitchen range,
or the stamp of a boot on a whitewashed floor
and memory makes my smile turn strange.

My heart in a thousand bits lies shattered
like broken ice on the water's face,
like a heap of stones you've knocked and scattered
or a virgin fallen in disgrace.

I shall leave this town as soon as I can;
sharp the stone here, deep the dung;
there's nothing of value here for a man
but the heavy word from everyone's tongue.

BRENDAN KENNELLY

The Thatcher

He whittled scallops for a hardy thatch,
His palm and fingers hard as the bog oak.
You'd see him of an evening, crouched
Under a tree, testing a branch. If it broke
He grunted in contempt and flung it away,
But if it stood the stretch, his sunken blue
Eyes briefly smiled. Then with his long knife he
Chipped, slashed, pointed. The pile of scallops grew.

Astride a house on a promised day,
He rammed and patted scallops into place
Though wind cut his eyes till he seemed to weep.
Like a god after making a world, his face
Grave with the secret, he'd stare and say—
"Let the wind rip and the rain pelt. This'll keep."

The Swimmer

For him the Shannon opens
Like a woman.
He has stepped over the stones

And cut the water
With his body;
But this river does not bleed for

Any man. How easily
He mounts the waves, riding them
As though they

Whispered subtle invitations to his skin,
Conspiring with the sun
To offer him

A white, wet rhythm. The deep beneath
Gives full support
To the marriage of wave and heart.

The waves he breaks turn back to stare
At the repeated ceremony
And the hills of Clare

Witness the fluent weddings,
The flawless congregation,
The choiring foam that sings

To limbs which must, once more,
Rising and falling in the sun,
Return to shore.

Again he walks upon the stones,
A new music in his heart,
A river in his bones

Flowing forever through his head
Private as a grave
Or as the bridal bed.

Bread

Someone else cut off my head
In a golden field.
Now I am re-created

By her fingers. This
Moulding is more delicate
Than a first kiss,

More deliberate than her own
Rising up
And lying down.

Even at my weakest, I am
Finer than anything
In this legendary garden

Yet I am nothing till
She runs her fingers through me
And shapes me with her skill.

The form that I shall bear
Grows round and white.
It seems I comfort her

Even as she slits my face
And stabs my chest.
Her feeling for perfection is

Absolute.
So I am glad to go through fire
And come out

Shaped like her dream.
In my way
I am all that can happen to men.
I came to life at her fingerends.
I will go back into her again.

Proof

I would like all things to be free of me,
Never to murder the days with presupposition,
Never to feel they suffer the imposition
Of having to be this or that. How easy
It is to maim the moment
With expectation, to force it to define
Itself. Beyond all that I am, the sun
Scatters its light as though by accident.

The fox eats its own leg in the trap
To go free. As it limps through the grass
The earth itself appears to bleed.
When the morning light comes up
Who knows what suffering midnight was?
Proof is what I do not need.

SEAMUS HEANEY

The Badgers

When the badger glimmered away
into another garden
you stood, half-lit with whiskey,
sensing you had disturbed
some soft returning.

The murdered dead,
you thought.
But could it not have been
some violent shattered boy
nosing out what got mislaid
between the cradle and the explosion,
evenings when windows stood open
and the compost smoked down the backs?

Visitations are taken for signs.
At a second house I listened
for duntings under the laurels
and heard intimations whispered
about being vaguely honoured.

And to read even by carcasses
the badgers have come back.
One that grew notorious
lay untouched in the roadside.
Last night one had me braking
but more in fear than in honour.

Cool from the sett and redolent
of his runs under the night,
the bogey of fern country
broke cover in me
for what he is:
pig family
and not at all what he's painted.

How perilous is it to choose
not to love the life we're shown?
His sturdy dirty body
and interloping grovel.
The intelligence in his bone.
The unquestionable houseboy's shoulders
that could have been my own.

The Skunk

Up, black, striped and damasked like the chasuble
At a funeral mass, the skunk's tail
Paraded the skunk. Night after night
I expected her like a visitor.

The refrigerator whinnied into silence.
My desk light softened beyond the verandah.
Small oranges bloomed in the orange tree.
I began to be tense as a voyeur.

After eleven years I was composing
Love-letters again, broaching the word "wife"
Like a stored cask, as if its slender vowel
Had mutated into the night earth and air

Of California. The beautiful, useless
Tang of eucalyptus spelt your absence.
The aftermath of a mouthful of wine
Was like inhaling you off a cold pillow.

And there she was, the intent and glamorous,
Ordinary, mysterious skunk,
Mythologized, demythologized,
Snuffing the boards five feet beyond me.

It all came back to me last night, stirred
By the sootfall of your things at bedtime,
Your head-down, tail-up hunt in a bottom drawer
For the black plunge-line nightdress.

The Otter

When you plunged
The light of Tuscany wavered
And swung through the pool
From top to bottom.

I loved your wet head and smashing crawl,
Your fine swimmer's back and shoulders
Surfacing and surfacing again
This year and every year since.

I sat dry-throated on the warm stones.
You were beyond me.
The mellowed clarities, the grape-deep air
Thinned and disappointed.

Thank God for the slow loadening.
When I hold you now
We are close and deep
As the atmosphere on water.

My two hands are plumbed water.
You are my palpable, lithe
Otter of memory
In the pool of the moment,

Turning to swim on your back,
Each silent, thigh-shaking kick
Re-tilting the light,
Heaving the cool at your neck.

And suddenly you're out,
Back again, intent as ever,
Heavy and frisky in your freshened pelt,
Printing the stones.

A Strange House

Racoons, soft-footed scavengers,
Hustled at the trash-can:
From the blond household timbers,
A whiff of indolent resin.

I sensed hubris of the body
Off steel and sanded grain,
The deliberate nudity
Of a beautiful hard woman.

We whose rooms were hide
And seek, valences and screens—
We were on the wrong side
Of those high, uncurtained panes.

A bare moon stared in
When we put out the light.
Listen.
Trees breathed upon that night

Were clandestine
As our first wedded work,
My eager scavenging,
Your cold nose in the dark.

A Dream of Jealousy

Walking with you and another lady
In wooded parkland, the whispering grass
Ran its fingers through our guessing silence
And the trees opened into a shady
Unexpected clearing where we sat down.
I think the candour of the light dismayed us.
We talked about desire and being jealous,

Our conversation a loose single gown
Or a white tablecloth spread out
Like a book of manners in the wilderness.
"Show me," I said to our companion, "what
I have much coveted, your breast's mauve star."
And she consented. O neither these verses
Nor my prudence, love, can heal your wounded stare.

Leavings

A soft whoosh, the sunset blaze
of straw on blackened stubble,
a thatch-deep, freshening,
barbarous crimson burn—

I rode down England
as they fired the crop
that was the leavings of a crop,
the smashed tow-coloured barley,

down from Ely's Lady Chapel,
the sweet tenor latin
forever banished,
the sumptuous windows

threshed clear by Thomas Cromwell.
Which circle does he tread,
scalding on cobbles,
each one a broken statue's head?

After midnight, after summer,
to walk in a sparking field,
to smell dew and ashes
and start Will Brangwen's ghost

from the hot soot—
a breaking sheaf of light,
abroad in the hiss
and clash of stooking.

MICHAEL LONGLEY

In Mayo

1

For her sake once again I disinter
Imagination like a brittle skull
From where the separating vertebrae
And scapulae litter a sandy wind,

As though to reach her I must circle
This burial mound, its shadow turning
Under the shadow of a seabird's wing:
A sundial for the unhallowed soul.

2

Though the townland's all ears, all eyes
To decipher our movements, she and I
Appear on the scene at the oddest times:
We follow the footprints of animals,

Then vanish into the old wives' tales
Leaving behind us landmarks to be named
After our episodes, and the mushrooms
That cluster where we happen to lie.

3

When it is time for her to fall asleep
And I touch her eyelids, may night itself,
By my rule of thumb, be no profounder
Than the grassy well among irises

Where wild duck shelter their candid eggs:
No more beguiling than a gull's feather
In whose manifold gradations of light
I clothe her now and erase the scene.

4

Dawns and dusks here should consist of
Me scooping a hollow for her hip-bone,
The stony headland a bullaun, a cup
To balance her body in like water:

Then a slow awakening to the swans
That fly home in twos, married for life,
Larks nestling beside the cattle's feet
And snipe the weight of the human soul.

The Goose

Remember the white goose in my arms,
A present still. I plucked the long
Flight-feathers, down from the breast,
Finest fuzz from underneath the wings.

I thought of you through the operation
And covered the unmolested head,
The pink eyes that had persisted in
An expression of disappointment.

It was right to hesitate before
I punctured the skin, made incisions
And broached with my reluctant fingers
The chill of its intestines, because

Surviving there, lodged in its tract,
Nudging the bruise of the orifice
Was the last egg. I delivered it
Like clean bone, a seamless cranium.

Much else followed which, for your sake,
I bundled away, burned on the fire
With the head, the feet, the perfect wings.
The goose was ready for the oven.

I would boil the egg for your breakfast,
Conserve for weeks the delicate fats
As in the old days. In the meantime
We dismantled it, limb by limb.

Ars Poetica

1

Because they are somewhere in the building
I'll get in touch with them, the wife and kids—
Or I'm probably a widower by now,
Divorced and here by choice, on holiday
And paying through the nose for it: a queue
Of one outside the bathroom for ever
And no windows with a view of the sea.

2

I am writing a poem at the office desk
Or else I am forging business letters—
What I am really up to, I suspect,
Is seducing the boss's secretary
Among the ashtrays on the boardroom table
Before absconding with the petty cash box
And a one way ticket to Katmandu.

3

I go disguised as myself, my own beard
Changed by this multitude of distortions
To stage whiskers, my hair a give-away,
A cheap wig, and my face a mask only—
So that, on entering the hall of mirrors
The judge will at once award the first prize
To me and to all of my characters.

4

After I've flown my rickety bi-plane
Under the Arc de Triomphe and before

I perform a double back-somersault
Without the safety net and—if there's time—
Walk the high wire between two waterfalls,
I shall draw a perfect circle free-hand
And risk my life in a final gesture.

5

Someone keeps banging the side of my head
Who is well aware that it's his furore,
His fists and feet I most want to describe—
My silence to date neither invitation
Nor complaint, but a stammering attempt
Once and for all to get him down in words
And allow him to push an open door.

6

I am on general release now, having
Put myself in the shoes of all husbands,
Dissipated my substance in the parlours
Of an entire generation and annexed
To my territory gardens, allotments
And the desire—even at this late stage—
To go along with the world and his wife.

SEAMUS DEANE

Migration

Someone is migrating.
He is going to the fifth
Season where he can hear
The greenness planning its leaves
And the landbreaks and the water
Co-ordinating the moment of foam.
He is going to seek his parents,
Looking in the history of their bodies
For what he inherited. He is migrating
Out of his nativities,
His tongue still undelivered, waiting
To be born in the word home.

Fording the River

Sunday afternoon and the water
Black among the stones, the forest
Ash-grey in its permanent dusk
Of unquivering pine. That day
You unexpectedly crossed the river.

It was cold and you quickly shouted
As your feet felt the wet white stones
Knocking together. I had bent
To examine a strand of barbed wire
Looping up from a buried fence

When I heard you shout. And,
There you were, on the other side,

Running away. In a slow puncturing
Of anticipation I shivered
As if you had, unpermitted, gone forever.

Gone, although you were already in the middle
Coming back; I picked up
Your shoes with a sense that years
Had suddenly decided to pass.
I remembered your riddle

On the way up here. '"Brother or sister
I have none, but that man's father
Is my father's son." Who am I
Talking about?' About my son,
Who crossed cold Lethe, thought it Rubicon.

The Brethren

Arraigned by silence, I recall
The noise of lecture-rooms,
School refectories and dining hall,
A hundred faces in a hundred spoons,
Raised in laughter or in prayer bent,
Each distorted and each innocent.

Torrential sunlight falling through the slats
Made marquetries of light upon the floor.
I still recall those greasy Belfast flats
Where parties hit upon a steady roar
Of subdued violence and lent
Fury to the Sabbath which we spent

Hung over empty streets where Jimmy Witherspoon
Sang under the needle old laments
Of careless love and the indifferent moon,
Evoked the cloudy drumbrush scents
Of Negro brothels while our Plymouth Brethren,
Two doors down, sat sunk in heaven.

Stupor Sunday, *stupor mundi.* What was to come?
The plaints that were growing
Their teeth in the jaws of their aquarium
Sunday's splashless, deep-sown
Peace? What if it were shattered?
Our noise was life and life mattered.

Recently I found old photographs
Fallen behind the attic water-tank
And saw my friends were now the staffs
Of great bureaucracies. Some frames stank
Of mildew, some were so defaced
That half the time I couldn't put a face

On half of them. Some were dead.
The water had seeped through a broken housing,
Had slowly savaged all those eyes and heads.
I felt its rusted coldness dousing
Those black American blues-fired tunes,
The faces echoed in those hammered spoons.

MICHAEL HARTNETT

Prisoners

brave
to keep in capture
whom he loved, this wild woman
not so old, so many years
in quiet place
unknown to all the town.
so her face was white as almond
pale as wax for lack of sunlight
blue skin by her eyes in etchings,
all her beauty now attainted,
all her loveliness unwanted.
   not to say his love was lessened:
   no: he came home to her same altar
   at night, grey horse bore him to the threshold,
   quiet rooms, where the woman sang her service,
   sang to new gods, to the church of her invention
   her own cloistered psalms, in her bishoped dress of scarlet.
for she built walls to keep God in,
and waiting there from eyes ahide
at night before her tearful face
at calm crossroads her child did raise,
her child into the secret world.
   and she involved a secret Lord,
   prayed the holy prayers she made herself,
   and sang so: my Lord God is a human Lord
   not Lord of towns, but Lord of white horses, holy
   of the hyacinth, the human Lord of light, of rain.
yes, Lord of sacred anguish, hear
me, and speak in rain of trees: send
your holy fire to heat me. I
cry: my Lord of holy pain, hear.
   house of slated roof was their house
   daylight knew no way to hound them
      out of peace:

the door was closed with iron chains
locked safe inside an open moat
         of water:
secret in their love they lived there:
the birch-hid dove was silk with peace.

Death of an Irishwoman

Ignorant, in the sense
she ate monotonous food
and thought the world was flat,
and pagan, in the sense
she knew the things that moved
at night were neither dogs nor cats
but púcas and darkfaced men
she nevertheless had fierce pride.
But sentenced in the end
to eat thin diminishing porridge
in a stone-cold kitchen
she clinched her brittle hands
around a world
she could not understand.
I loved her from the day she died.
She was a summer dance at the crossroads.
She was a cardgame where a nose was broken.
She was a song that nobody sings.
She was a house ransacked by soldiers.
She was a language seldom spoken.
She was a child's purse, full of useless things.

from *A Farewell to English*

for Brendan Kennelly

i.

Her eyes were coins of porter and her West
Limerick voice talked velvet in the house:

her hair was black as the glossy fireplace
wearing with grace her Sunday-night-dance best.
She cut the froth from glasses with a knife
and hammered golden whiskies on the bar
and her mountainy body tripped the gentle
mechanism of verse: the minute interlock
of word and word began, the rhythm formed.
I sunk my hands into tradition
sifting the centuries for words. This quiet
excitement was not new: emotion challenged me
to make it sayable. The clichés came
at first, like matchsticks snapping from the world
of work: mánla, séimh, dubhfholtach, álainn, caoin:
they came like grey slabs of slate breaking from
an ancient quarry, mánla, séimh, dubhfholtach,
álainn, caoin, slowly vaulting down the dark
unused escarpments, mánla, séimh, dubhfholtach,
álainn, caoin, crashing on the cogs, splinters
like axeheads damaging the wheels, clogging
the intricate machine, mánla, séimh,
dubhfholtach, álainn, caoin. Then Pegasus
pulled up, the girth broke and I was flung back
on the gravel of Anglo-Saxon.
What was I doing with these foreign words?
I, the polisher of the complex clause,
wizard of grasses and warlock of birds
midnight-oiled in the metric laws?

ii.

Half afraid to break a promise
made to Dinny Halpin Friday night
I sat down from my walk to Camas
Sunday evening, Doody's Cross,
and took off my burning boots
on a gentle bench of grass.
The cows had crushed the evening
green with mint
springwater from the roots
of a hawkfaced firtree on my right

Part I. *dubhfholtach:* blacklocked. *álainn:* beautiful. *mánla, séimh* and *caoin:*
words whose meanings hover about the English adjectives graceful, gentle.

swamped pismires bringing home
their sweet supplies
and strawberries looked out
with ferret's eyes.
These old men walked on the summer road
sugán belts and long black coats
with big ashplants and half-sacks
of rags and bacon on their backs.
They stopped before me with a knowing look
hungry, snotnosed, half-drunk.
I said grand evening
and they looked at me awhile
then took their roads
to Croom, Meentogues and Cahirmoyle.
They looked back once,
black moons of misery
sickling their eye-sockets,
a thousand years of history
in their pockets.

. . .

v.

I say farewell to English verse,
to those I found in English nets:
my Lorca holding out his arms
to love the beauty of his bullets,
Pasternak who outlived Stalin
and died because of lesser beasts:
to all the poets I have loved
from Wyatt to Robert Browning:
to Father Hopkins in his crowded grave
and to our bugbear Mr. Yeats
who forced us into exile
on islands of bad verse.

Part II. Croom: area in Co. Limerick associated with Andrias Mac Craith (d. 1795); also, seat of the last 'courts' of Irish (Gaelic) poetry; also, my birthplace. Meentogues: birthplace of Aodhagán Ó'Rathaille. Cahirmoyle: site of the house of John Bourke (fl. 1690), patron of Dáibhí O Bruadair.

Among my living friends
there is no poet I do not love,
although some write
with bitterness in their hearts:
they are one art, our many arts.
Poets with progress
make no peace or pact:
the act of poetry
is a rebel act.

vii.

This road is not new.
I am not a maker of new things.
I cannot hew
out of the vacuumcleaner minds
the sense of serving dead kings.

I am nothing new.
I am not a lonely mouth
trying to chew
a niche for culture
in the clergy-cluttered south.

But I will not see
great men go down
who walked in rags
from town to town
finding English a necessary sin
the perfect language to sell pigs in.

I have made my choice
and leave with little weeping:
I have come with meagre voice
to court the language of my people.

DEREK MAHON

Ford Manor

Non sapei tu che qui è l'uom felice?

Even on the quietest days the distant
Growl of cars remains persistent,
Reaching us in this airy box
We share with the fieldmouse and the fox;
But she drifts in maternity blouses
Among crack-paned greenhouses—
A smiling Muse come back to life,
Part child, part mother, and part wife.

Even on the calmest nights the fitful
Prowl of planes is seldom still
Where Gatwick tilts to guide them home
From Tokyo, New York or Rome;
Yet even this morning Earth disposes
Bluebells, roses and primroses,
The dawn throat-whistle of a thrush
Deep in the dripping lilac bush.

Penshurst Place

And if these pleasures may thee move . . .

The bright drop quivering on a thorn
In the rich silence after rain,
Lute music from the orchard aisles,
The paths ablaze with daffodils,
Intrigue and venery in the air
A l'ombre des jeunes filles en fleurs,
The iron hand and the velvet glove—
Come live with me and be my love.

A pearl face, numinously bright,
Shining in silence of the night,
A muffled crash of smouldering logs,
Bad dreams of courtiers and of dogs,
The Spanish ships around Kinsale,
The screech owl and the nightingale,
The falcon and the turtle dove—
Come live with me and be my love.

Please

I built my house
in a forest far
from the venal roar.

Somebody please
beat a path
to my door.

The Return

for John Hewitt

I am saying goodbye to the trees,
The beech, the cedar, the elm,
The mild woods of these parts
Misted with car exhaust,
And sawdust, and the last
Gasps of the poisoned nymphs.

I have watched girls walking
And children playing under
Lilac and rhododendron,

And me flicking my ash
Into the rose bushes
As if I owned the place;

As if the trees responded
To my ignorant admiration
Before dawn when the branches
Glitter at first light,
Or later on when the finches
Disappear for the night;

And often thought if I lived
Long enough in this house
I would turn into a tree
Like somebody in Ovid
—A small tree certainly
But a tree nonetheless—

Perhaps befriend the oak,
The chestnut and the yew,
Become a home for birds,
A shelter for the nymphs,
And gaze out over the downs
As if I belonged here too.

But where I am going the trees
Are few and far between.
No richly forested slopes,
Not for a long time,
And few winking woodlands;
There are no nymphs to be seen.

Out there you would look in vain
For a rose bush; but find,
Rooted in stony ground,
A last stubborn growth
Battered by constant rain
And twisted by the sea-wind

With nothing to recommend it
But its harsh tenacity

Between the blinding windows
And the forests of the sea,
As if its very existence
Were a reason to continue.

Crone crow, scarecrow,
Its worn fingers scrabbling
At a torn sky, it stands
On the edge of everything
Like a burnt-out angel
Raising petitionary hands.

Grotesque by day, at twilight
An almost tragic figure
Of anguish and despair,
It merges into the funeral
Cloud-continent of night
As if it belongs there.

Surrey Poems

1. Midsummer

Today the longest day and the people have gone.
The sun concentrates on the kitchen garden
with the bright intensity of June.
The birds I heard singing at dawn
are dozing among the leaves
while a faint soap waits its turn
in a blue sky, strange to the afternoon—
one eye on the pasture where cows roam
and one on the thin line between land
and sea, where the quietest waves
will break there when the people have gone home.

2. Field Bath

Ancient bathtub in the fallow field—
midges, brown depths where once
the ladies soaped their thighs.
Now cow faces, clouds,
starlight, nobody there.

Nobody there for days and nights
but my own curious thoughts
out there on their own
in a rainstorm or before dawn
peering over the rim
and sending nothing back to my warm room.

3. Dry Hill

The grass falls silent and the trees cease
when my shoes go swishing there.
Vetch, thyme, cowslip,
whatever your names are,
there is no need for fear,
I am only looking. Perhaps
that is what you are afraid of.

Did I tell you about my grandparents,
how they slaved all their lives
and for what? Did I tell you
about the lot of women,
the eyes of children?
Did I tell you the one about?

Please yourselves, at least I tried,
I have a right to be here too.
Maybe not like you;
like the birds,
say, or the wind blowing through.

EILÉAN NÍ CHUILLEANÁIN

Swineherd

"When all this is over," said the swineherd,
"I mean to retire, where
Nobody will have heard about my special skills
And conversation is mainly about the weather.

I intend to learn how to make coffee, at least as well
As the Portuguese lay-sister in the kitchen
And polish the brass fenders every day.
I want to lie awake at night
Listening to cream crawling to the top of the jug
And the water lying soft in the cistern.

I want to see an orchard where the trees grow in straight lines
And the yellow fox finds shelter between the navy-blue trunks,
Where it gets dark early in summer
And the apple-blossom is allowed to wither on the bough."

Deaths and Engines

We came down above the houses
In a stiff curve, and
At the edge of Paris airport
Saw an empty tunnel
—The back half of a plane, black
On the snow, nobody near it,
Tubular, burnt-out and frozen.

When we faced again
The snow-white runways in the dark

151

No sound came over
The loudspeakers, except the sighs
Of the lonely pilot.

The cold of metal wings is contagious:
Soon you will need wings of your own,
Cornered in the angle where
Time and life like a knife and fork
Cross, and the lifeline in your palm
Breaks, and the curve of an aeroplane's track
Meets the straight skyline.

The images of relief:
Hospital pyjamas, screens round a bed
A man with a bloody face
Sitting up in bed, conversing cheerfully
Through cut lips:
These will fail you some time.

One day you will find yourself alone
Accelerating down a blind
Alley, too late to stop
And know how light your death is,
How serious the survival of the others.
You will be scattered like wreckage;
The pieces, every one a different shape
Will painfully lodge in the hearts
Of everybody who loves you.

The Lady's Tower

Hollow my high tower leans
Back to the cliff; my thatch
Converses with spread sky,
Heronries. The grey wall
Slices downward and meets
A sliding flooded stream
Pebble-banked, small diving
Birds. Downstairs my cellars plumb.

Behind me shifting the oblique veins
Of the hill; my kitchen is damp,
Spiders shaded under brown vats.

I hear the stream change pace, glance from the stove
To see the punt is now floating freely
Bobs square-ended, the rope dead-level.

Opening the kitchen door
The quarry brambles miss my hair
Sprung so high their fruit wastes.

And up the tall stairs my bed is made
Even with a sycamore root
At my small square window.

All night I lie sheeted, my broom chases down treads
Delighted spirals of dust: the yellow duster glides
Over shelves, around knobs: bristle stroking flagstone
Dancing with the spiders around the kitchen in the dark
While cats climb the tower and the river fills
A spoonful of light on the cellar walls below.

Odysseus Meets the Ghosts of the Women

There also he saw
The celebrated women
And in death they looked askance;
He stood and faced them,
Shadows flocked by the dying ram
To sup the dark blood flowing at his heel
—His long sword fending them off,
Their whispering cold
Their transparent grey throats from the lifeblood.

He saw the daughters, wives
Mothers of heroes or upstanding kings

The longhaired goldbound women who had died
Of pestilence, famine, in slavery
And still queens but they did not know
His face, even Anticleia
His own mother. He asked her how she died
But she passed by his elbow, her eyes asleep.

The hunter still followed
Airy victims, and labour
Afflicted even here the cramped shoulders—
The habit of distress.

A hiss like thunder, all their voices
Broke on him; he fled
For the long ship, the evening sea
Persephone's poplars
And her dark willow trees.

A Gentleman's Bedroom

Those long retreating shades,
A river of roofs inclining
In the valley side. Gables and stacks
And spires, with trees tucked between them:
All graveyard shapes
Viewed from his high windowpane.

A coffin-shaped looking-glass replies,
Soft light, polished, smooth as fur,
Blue of mown grass on a lawn,
With neckties crookedly doubled over it.

Opening the door, all walls point at once to the bed
Huge red silk in a quarter of the room
Knots drowning in deep mahogany
And uniform blue volumes shelved at hand.

And a desk calendar, a fountain-pen,
A weighty table-lighter in green marble,
A cigar-box, empty but dusted,
A framed young woman in a white dress
Indicate the future from the cold mantel.

The house sits silent,
The shiny linoleum
Would creak if you stepped on it.
Outside it is still raining
But the birds have begun to sing.

PAUL DURCAN

The Difficulty That Is Marriage

We disagree to disagree, we divide, we differ;
Yet each night as I lie in bed beside you
And you are faraway curled up in sleep
I array the moonlit ceiling with a mosaic of question-marks;
How was it I was so lucky to have ever met you?
I am no brave pagan proud of my mortality
Yet gladly on this changeling earth I should live for ever
If it were with you, my sleeping friend.
I have my troubles and I shall always have them
But I should rather live with you for ever
Than exchange my troubles for a changeless kingdom.
But I do not put you on a pedestal or throne;
You must have your faults but I do not see them.
If it were with you, I should live for ever

The Weeping Headstones
of the Isaac Becketts

The Protestant graveyard was a forbidden place
So naturally as children we explored its precincts;
Clambered over drystone walls under elms and chestnuts,
Parted long grasses and weeds, poked about under yews,
Reconnoitred the chapel whose oak doors were always closed,
Stared at the schist headstones of the Isaac Becketts.
And then we would depart with mortal sins in our bones
As ineradicable as an arthritis
But we had seen enough to know what the old folks meant
When we would overhear them whisperingly at night refer to
"The headstones of the Becketts—they would make you weep".

These arthritises of sin:
But although we had only six years each on our backs
We could decipher
Brand-new roads open up through heaven's fields
And upon them—like thousands upon thousands
Of people kneeling in the desert—
The weeping headstones of the Isaac Becketts

The Kilfenora Teaboy

I'm the Kilfenora teaboy
And I'm not so very young
But though the land is going to pieces
I will not take up the gun;
I am happy making tea
I make lots of it when I can
And when I can't—I just make do
And I do a small bit of sheepfarming on the side

Oh but it's the small bit of furze between two towns
Is what makes the Kilfenora teaboy really run

I have nine healthy daughters
And please God I will have more
Sometimes my dear wife beats me
But on the whole she's a gentle soul;
When I'm not making her some tea
I sit out and watch them all
Ring-a-rosying in the street
And I do a small bit of sheepfarming on the side

Oh but it's the small bit of furze between two towns
Is what makes the Kilfenora teaboy really run

Oh indeed my wife is handsome
She has a fire lighting in each eye
You can pluck laughter from her elbows
And from her knees pour money's tears;

I make all my tea for her
I'm her teaboy on the hill
And I also thatch her roof
And I do a small bit of sheepfarming on the side

Oh but it's the small bit of furze between two towns
Is what makes the Kilfenora teaboy really run

And I'm not only a famous teaboy
I'm a famous caveman too;
I paint pictures by the hundred
But you can't sell walls;
Although the people praise my pictures
As well as my turf-perfumèd blend
They rarely fling a fiver in my face;
Oh don't we do an awful lot of dying on the side

But Oh it's the small bit of furze between two towns
Is what makes the Kilfenora teaboy really run

JOHN ENNIS

Corbetstown

1

Cousin, I visit you, James Gorman, for you have died,
Wake your father, sods of fire, house in Corbetstown.
Football under giant oaks, quiet industry, fieldlove confide
Delights no more or care to farm they cannot own.
Your well gave yearly in Augusts when neighbours ran dry,
I saw Bannons rope up crystal from that deep spring.
Hall door's raw wood again. Latch opens on a piggery.
Deeper than vixen earthed you hear no swallows sing.

2

Years ago, trip to you, disentangle of roads, perpetual
Bridges, branching south on a country lane loosed joy.
Today, I'd ungloom May's white chestnut blossoms, natural
Welcome. By the door helloes petalled, a man, a boy.
On these a single lightning bolt scored a direct hit
Brought low Connemara pony, the trap, limbed family
Guinea fowl pirouetting grey speckled blue on old Tom Gorman's wit,
Sundays we'd clip-clop off, great spirits, cheer Offaly.

3

Hearth of firechairs. The black turf blaze no time let out.
Nooked in the kitchen, an old radio fed on two wet batteries
Throbbed to Korea War, boxing bouts, Gaelic matches. Fear and doubt
Sprawled nightly to Our Lady's soft ritual flatteries.
Next room, decanters sat twinned in oak-stained cabinets
Guarded port for visitors, a dead wife's wedding delf,
Two pale cold-boned festive dinner service sets.
A mantel clock tick-tocked so sedately to itself.

4

Applause reared me. Chores after supper. Holidays,
I helped Tom, white thatch, scalded late milk pails,

Sat them all together for the dawn. Out of our daze,
Mists, summer sleep he'd lift us, trot us brisk tales
To Castlejordan by trap for sweets, a page of groceries.
Gun sombred his limed dairy. Tide of the Troubles did rouse
Him once. "Give us the gun, Gorman," hissed seas.
But he flushed out the small abusive Cains round the house.

5

Swallows' reverie fills sky, flits docks, nettles of the yard.
Music blasts five farms away, Sunday carnival off at Rhode,
Afternoon of merry-go-round faces. James, here, it's hard
Watching love shake down, a frail crumble of filial code.
Yesterday, two lizards, we'd scale the mortar of this old barn wall.
Runnels, berried ivy it was. First climb, my fear you seized
Dragged me up. To-day there's no gable at all.
Memory, other sheds' blood-rust too filters dry light in nailed galvanized.

6

Swallows couple, weave derelicts. Unhasping the yard gate
I step into starveling grass new owner soon will mow.
At my face there drift lazy crows, crows that striate
Sky's sultry August, or, beak-gaping, writhe meadow.
James, laughing, once, one sun-driven cloudless June
We trod corn here, sundown, dew. Green of adolescence
You illustrated to me. Oak thrushes raged in tune
Emblazoned an hour or two in leaves above the lane fence.

7

Hedges next field smoulder, tower a sullen fifteen feet high,
Canopy your mangold barrow upturned, thrown down a gripe.
Gorman-tilled corn clay grows rank, blooms wild to die,
Fosters cuckoo-spittle grubs. Poppies are starting to ripe.
Years auctioned, you fatten ragwort too. Thistles bolt to seed.
Praiseach jaundices good soil. This summer crop loss
Is consummate. White bindweed blossoms. Deep in heat-wild weed
I search waste for an hour, would find your sodden cross.

8

Farm-buyer appears over a clump of praiseach, nears me, is set
For words. Suspicious as an Alsation, he sniffs at my presence,

"Who're you? What brings you here? I don't think we've met?"
I tell him, James, you, cousin, seeded this field. His dense
Xenophobia falters, spits its phlegm onto a golden dandelion:
"The little fool—he stole his father's gun, at point blank range was shot
Hunting crows in the corn! Old Gorman's flame soon snuffed out—his
    only son
Dead! Move three steps to me! Now you're bang on the spot!"

9

"Stretched at your feet the Gorman lad lay. Young Bannon shot his guts
    away."
I lean upon a gorgon, woolgather. Maybe life sleeps in a stone.
July 16th flew by, your fifteenth birthday, sunny death-day.
James Mary, it was feast of Mt. Carmel. You grew up on loan
To virgin clay, grave yawned. Make horse sense of the sun,
Trap, gloomy arcades of the sky. Crows, wounded, flew
A few yards off. You threw Seán Bannon the Troubles' gun,
Jumped to sprint after crows. Seán miscaught the gun, killed you.

10

Death in the turning oats. Well, so Life ebbs, companion goes.
Seán ran pale, hotfoot off home. Fact lashed him with its rod.
Double-barrel tremens kicked him speechless. Poor Van Gogh sounds his
    crows,
Daubed tears. Seán's people raised you, stanched vivid blood,
Carried mute stereo into kitchen. Doctor motored from Edenderry.
Father traipsed after you to inquest, mortuary, the funeral's
Lowering down. The green-gold corn had drained you dry.
Walk back to the house with me. Touch your webbed socketless walls.

11

"I like to bed my Landrace sow below! You see, she's a free trot
Of all the downstairs rooms," the owner laughs. "A drink?
Come on, join with me in one!" Swallows twitter. "My brother got
Cancer last year, felt the knife. St. Luke's made me think,
Boy! Heart's a ton weight since. Bitch runs!" He plucks a door rose,
Scrolls an IFA FIGHT SCOUR. I speak of pros and cons.
A shadow stretches on us. He sparks to his fusty hay rows
Crying, "O Christ, I wish I was married, had three sons!"

12

Time for me to leave too. I pledge litter of yard scene
Verse, weedy rivulet over which we drove your dairy cows
To stable, strewn happiness of play, swings, age was to wean
Us of. Dismay of tackling, axles, coulterless ploughs
(I could pray a miracle, you to burst outdoors, restore these things)
Crawling like limbless cripples toward your flagstone.
Yes, I could pour you fizzy resurrectionade, wind the Easter Bird that
      sings,
St. John's Day cutter blades, toy a Rite of Spring unison.

13

What was of you is no more. The dapple-grey rocking horse,
That forbidden junk room, its random ecstasies upstairs
Like tentacles round us, our bed, the bewildering morse
Of stars and moon, the window's cold-stoked universal fires.
One day the sunlit oval mirror fell in the parlour
Shattered face, mantel clock, time. A farrowing sow
Knocks about day in, day out, on us, uproots floor,
Suckles her blind piglets in your hacked rooms now.

14

Our rough-and-tumble football shouldering in the hall
A wet foggy twilight overtaxed your father's patience,
Drowned his spilt news. Toll of Koreans, U.S. meant damn all.
Forgetting us, out in swathes, owner races the sky's turbulence
Cocking hay, landman struggling like your dead father.
I saw Tom bleed for you, curse guns. Less of a man,
Blood blackened, thinned in him. Aftergrass weather
He'd ramble fields, plod wraith-alive, a zoo-caged pelican.

15

A three-century old yellow clay wall festered with wild bees.
On hunkers by a clipped hedge we pelted them with turf clods.
Father lit at our backs. Tongue hurt us. Demure as geese
You, I stood. Today Gorman's flowering tree, hearthstone gods
Approach ash in other fires. Yet, I do not think of rooms
Destined to be cold troughs of auction, haunts of swine
Lightning lingers on now, nor of the clay-dribbling womb's
Desolation, but where bees sucked, frail words combine.

The Croppy Boy

It's no use, your wild nightly haggle, horse-pissed over me
At Passage by the Suir or maudlin down in Dungannon stoned.
The piked suns shine on ever more cruelly watery.
Winy streets we littered are innocently crimsoned.

On wet cobbles to the sweaty rope, you'll halo me. Naïve,
O yes, my blond teenage hair is styled like the French.
I'm not crying. To ladies, prance of Hessians, I clench
My bony dream, walk on. My ignorant head's a bee-hive.

From their suite rooms the yogurt mouths of hypocrites
Spit me out like bile. No lusty Patrick sucks their tits.

Rousing Christ, ladies do with me what they please.
While I die, blackbirds sing up the fat-arsed trees.

Mother, It's cruel. Yeomen bar us any last good-bye.
Yesterday I danced, tapped a jig. Noon, see me die.

Alice of Daphne, 1799

I am Alice of Daphne, and my heart clogs for John Pounden.
   As the stag cornered by pitch-forks, so antlered his thought
against the Croppies.
   As the Jonathan amongst scented trees of the orchard, so rose
my sweet back in Daphne. I knew a tender spot down under his
branches, basked long among his juicy apples.
   He rushed me the road to Enniscorthy, I was far gone, awkward with our loving:
   Bed me with slovens, madden me with fiddles, I grow big
now, sick for Daphne.
   His trunk leant gently onto mine, for I was fourteen years of
age.

*

And I said, Never, Never shall we be torn asunder or cut off from petalled Daphne, though our green hills crawl black with Croppies like flies, for I will not unloose that daft chase wreathing our laurels up the sloped white blossoms.

I grafted and shall graft, Jonathan, my virgin bones to yours.

McGuire, good tenant, coffined you when we stank Enniscorthy where Croppies piked the brave Orange.

*

John was twenty-one under the fruiting tree. I played the skittery dove after his apples.

Look, my lovelies, the mason plumbs our Wall! You can walk by the Slaney!

Crocus open on the Spring Lawn. On Vinegar Hill Providence stooped and smiled and picked but a few of the Croppies.

The Black Prince plum blooms early this March for my dears, Mary, John Colley, Jane, Patrick, Fanny.

But poor baby Joshua is down with the fits.

EAVAN BOLAND

Song

Where in blind files
Bats outsleep the frost
Water slips through stones
Too fast, too fast
For ice; afraid he'd slip
By me I asked him first.

Round as a bracelet
Clasping the wet grass,
An adder drowsed by berries
Which change blood to cess;
Dreading delay's venom
I risked the first kiss.

My skirt in my hand,
Lifting the hem high
I forded the river there;
Drops splashed my thigh.
Ahead of me at last
He turned at my cry:

"Look how the water comes
Boldly to my side;
See the waves attempt
What you have never tried."
He late that night
Followed the leaping tide.

The Gorgon Child

I

It was the dark month
when ice delivers from the earth

crocus by quick crocus
snow's afterbirth.

I wove under the lights
my lace of sweat.
Lifted, I looked down
at the snaky wet

my legs beheaded,
the slick, forked tongues
of your head
and for a glance

I petrified with the season.
Little gorgon
how you marrowed stone
into me,

the bitter truth
that giving birth
was our division.
A skull cap

of forceps cauled
the python stings,
the ringlet coils.
I lay back

to a cluck of nuns,
to a stone knowing:
from now our meetings
would be mere re-unions.

II

I start awake
from a soft sleep,
from a dream of heels
under my heart.

You are somewhere else,
weeping the jungle language
of new hungers.
I am stone again.

The milk heats.
The bottle warmer
ticks itself off.
I lift you up.

You suck busily.
By the mercy
of the nursery light
we grow less apart,

among bears and rag dolls,
in their big shadows
we flesh
to warm fact.

Light contracts.
The world lives down
the dark
union of its wonders.

The milkman hums away
to his doorsteps,
his empties.
You smile

at the swinging tails
and cardboard whiskers
of the cat mobile.
Dawn sunders

to define:
As you are my horizon,
I your earth,
I cradle you and see

how by separations
love survives
its own stone hour,
its gorgon birth.

Menses

I am the moon's looking-glass.
My days are moon-dials.
She will never be done with me.
Her tides full and pulse.
They spill out of my eyes.

I am the foul pollution of her wake.
My months leash to her.
My waters crawl to her light:
a slick haul,
a fallen self,
a sort of hated daughter.

How I envy them!
These ruffians of my garden.
Even the meadowsweet.
Yes they are free of her.
They are streetwalkers,
lesbians,
nuns.
I am not one of them.

Each filament,
each anther bred
from its own style,
its stamen,
is to itself a christening,
and falls to earth

so ignorant
so innocent
of the sweated waters
and the watered salts,
of ecstasy and birth.

I am a womb away.

How they would pity me
tonight
when she comes
bitching out of trees,
looking for her looking-glass.
And it is me.

Yes it is me
she poaches her old face in,
me she bloats with her waters,
me she muddles with her blood,
and her stupidity will addle me:

so when I'm grown
round and obscene with child
or when I moan
for him between the sheets,
then I believe like her
that I am bright and original
and that my light's my own.

JOHN BANVILLE

Fragment from a Novel in Progress

JOHANNES KEPLER, ASLEEP in his ruff, has dreamt the solution to the cosmic mystery. He holds it cupped in his mind as in his hands he would a precious something of unearthly stillness and frailty. O do not wake! But he will. Mistress Barbara, with a grain of grim satisfaction, shook him per instructions by his ill-shod foot, and at once the fabulous egg burst, leaving only a bit of glair and a few shattered co-ordinates of curved shell.

He was cramped and cold. There was a vile gum of sleep in his mouth. Opening a murderous eye he spied his wife reaching for his foot again, and dealt her a tiny kick to the knuckles. She looked at him, and under that fat flushed look he winced and made elaborate business with the brim of his borrowed hat. The child Regina, his stepdaughter, primly perched beside her mother, took in this little skirmish with her accustomed mild gaze. Young Tyge Brahe appeared then, leaning down from on high, a pale moist melanochroid, lean of limb, limp of paw, with a sly eye.

'We are arrived, sir,' he said, smirking. That *sir*. The astronomer, wiping his fouled mouth discreetly on his sleeve alighted on quaking legs from the carriage.

'Ah.'

The castle of Benatek confronted him, grand and impassive in the sharp sunlit February air, more vast even than the black bulk of woe that had lowered over him all the way from Graz. A bubble of gloom rose and broke in the mud of his fuddled wits. Mastlin, even Mastlin had failed him: why expect more of Tycho the Dane? Tears that he dared not shed splintered his already poor vision. He was not yet thirty; he felt far older than that. . . . But then, knuckling his eyes, he turned in time to witness the Junker Tengnagel, caparisoned blond brute, falling arse over tip off his rearing horse into the rutted slush of the road, and he marvelled at the inexhaustible bounty of the world, that has always a little consolation to offer.

It was some comfort too to discover that the grand serenity of Benatek was confined to its stony interior: once inside the gates that gave on to a cobbled courtyard, the quintet of travellers found itself in the mist of bedlam. Large-scale alterations were in progress. Planks clattered, bricks crashed, masons whistled. An overburdened pack mule, ears back and muzzle turned inside out, brayed and brayed. Tyge waved a languid hand and said: 'The new Uraniborg,' and laughed and, as they passed under the sagging threat of a massive granite lintel, a surge of excitement, tinged with the vague aftertaste of his dream, rose like warm gorge in Kepler's throat. Perhaps after all he had done right in coming to Bohemia? He might do great work here, at Brahe's castle, swaddled in the folds of a personality larger far and madder than his own.

They entered a second, smaller courtyard. There were no workings here. Patches of pocked, copper-stained snow clung in crevices and on window ledges. A pale beam of sunlight leaned against a tawny wall. All was calm, or was until, like a thing dropped into a still pool, a figure suddenly appeared from under the shadow of an arch, a dwarf it was, tiny, with huge hands and head and little legs and a humped back. He smiled, showing teeth too big for the prim pink mouth, and essayed a curtsy as they went by. Frau Barbara giggled, and took Regina's hand.

'God save you, gentles,' the dwarf piped, in his miniature voice, and was ignored.

Through a studded door they entered a low dark hall with an open fire and many persons moving dimly about in the reddish gloom. Kepler hung back, his wife behind him panting softly in his ear. They peered. Could it be they had been led into the servants' quarters? At a table by the hearth sat a lean dark man with a moustache, hugely eating. Kepler's heart thumped: he had heard tell of Tycho Brahe's eccentricities, and doubtless it was one of them to dine down here, and doubtless this was he, the great man at last. It was not. The fellow looked up with a leer and said to Tycho's son: 'Well! you are finally returned. And how are things in Prague?'

Young Tyge shrugged. 'Chapped. I would think.'

'Eh? O, ha, I have you. Ha.' He glanced toward Tengnagel, who had strode straight, glowering, to the fire. 'What ails our broody friend?'

'A fall from his mount,' said Tyge.

'Yes? The trollops are so lively these days then, in town?'

Kepler began to fidget. Surely there should have been some more suitable reception that this: was he being deliberately slighted, or was it just the way of aristocrats? Should he assert his presence? That might be a gross failure of tact. But Frau Barbara would begin to nag him in a moment. Then something brushed against him and he twitched in fright. It was the dwarf, who planted himself before the astronomer and examined

with calm attention the troubled white face and myopic gaze, the frayed
breeches, crumpled ruff, the little pale claws clutching the plumed hat.
'Sir Mathematicus, I venture,' and bowed again; 'welcome, welcome indeed,' as if he were lord of the house.

'This,' said young Brahe, 'is Jeppe, my father's fool. It is a manner of
sacred beast, I warn you.'

The dwarf smiled, shaking his great smooth head. 'Tut, master, I am
but a poor maimed man, a nothing. But you are tardy, we have looked
for you and your—' he darted a glance at Kepler's wife '—baggage this
week past. Your daddy is fretting.'

Tyge frowned. 'Remember, you,' he said softly, 'shit-eating toad, one
day I will inherit you.'

Mistress Barbara bridled. Such talk! and in the child's hearing! She had
been for some time silently totting up against Benatek a score of particu-
lars that totalled now a general affront. 'Johannes,' she began, but just
then the dark diner rose from his table and announced: 'Well, I must be
off,' and tapping a long finger lightly on young Tyge's breastbone, 'Tell
him, your dad, I regret the loss of the elk, will you? He's wrought still,
and won't see me, but the affair was no fault of mine: the beast was
drunk. Anyway, farewell.' And nodding to the Keplers he went quickly
out, flinging the wing of his heavy cloak across his shoulder and clamping
his hat on his head. Kepler looked after him. Barbara prodded:
'Johannes.' Tyge had wandered off. Tengnagel brooded. 'Come,' said the
dwarf, and showed again, like something swiftly shown before being
palmed, his thin malevolent smile. He led them up dank flights of stairs,
along endless stone corridors. The castle resounded with vague shouts,
snatches of wild singing, a banging of doors. The guest rooms were cavernous and sparsely furnished. Barbara wrinkled her nose at the smell of
damp. The baggage, what there was of it, had not been brought up. Jeppe
the dwarf leaned in a doorway with arms folded, watching. Kepler retreated to the huge mullioned window and on tiptoe peered down upon
the courtyard and the workers and a cloaked figure cantering laboriously
toward the gates on a foreshortened horse. Despite misgivings he had in
his heart expected something large and lavish of Benatek: gold rooms and
spontaneous applause, the attention of magnificent serious people, light
and space and time; not this grey, these deformities, the mess and confusion of other lives, this familiar—O, familiar!—disorder.

*

Was Tycho Brahe himself not large, was he not lavish? Yet when
within the hour he was summoned to the presence, Kepler, instead of lift-

ing his spirit sufficiently up to meet this eminence, launched at once upon an account of his troubles, pained by the whining note in his voice and yet unable to suppress it. There was cause enough for whining, after all. The Dane of course, Kepler gloomily supposed, knew nothing of money worries and all that, these squalid matters. His vast calm was informed by centuries of aristocratic assurance. Even the room where they sat, high and light, with a fine old ceiling and a rich glow in the warm yellow stone of the walls, bespoke a solid grandeur. Here disorder would not dare show its leering fat face. Tycho himself, with his silence and his stare, his gleaming dome of skull and metal nose, seemed more than human, seemed a great weighty engine whose imperceptible workings were holding firmly in their courses all the disparate doings of the castle and its myriad lives.

'And although in Graz I had many persons of influence on my side, even the Jesuits, yes, it was to no avail, the papist authorities continued to hound me without mercy, and would have me renounce my faith, and even—you will not believe it sir—I was even forced to pay a fine of ten thalers for the privilege of burying my poor children by the Lutheran rite!'

Tycho stirred, and dealt his great moustaches a downward thrust of thumb and forefinger. Kepler fell silent and sat stooped with plaintive gaze as if the yoke of that finger and thumb had fallen upon his thin shoulders.

'What is your philosophy, sir?' the Dane asked.

Italian oranges throbbed in a pewter bowl on the table between them. Kepler had never seen oranges before. Blazoned, big with ripeness, they were uncanny in their tense inexorable thereness.

'I hold the world to be a manifestation of the possibility of order,' he said. That was another fragment of his dream. He was not sure what it meant. Tycho Brahe was looking at him again, stonily. 'That is,' he hastened, 'I espouse the natural philosophy.' He wished he had dressed differently. The ruff especially he regretted. It had been intended to make an impression, but ruffs were out of fashion, and anyway this one was too tight. His, or rather Baron Hoffman's, plumed hat languished on the floor at his feet, another brave but ill-judged flourish, with a dent in the crown where he had inadvertently stepped on it. Tycho, gazing reflectively at a far high corner of the room, said:

'When I came first to Bohemia the Emperor lodged us in Prague at the house of the late vice chancellor, where the infernal ringing of bells from the Capuchin monastery nearby was a torment night and day.' He shrugged. 'One has always to contend with disturbance.'

Kepler nodded gravely. Bells, yes; bells would seriously disturb the concentration, indeed, though not so seriously, he fancied, as the shrieking of one's children dying in meningeal agony. They had, he and this

Dane, a great deal to learn about each other. He glanced round then, with what was meant to be an ingratiating smile, envy in it, and admiration. 'But now, of course, here . . . ?' The wall by which they sat was almost all a vast high window of many leaded panes, that gave on to a prospect of vineyards and pasture land rolling away into blue pellucid distances. Winter sunlight blazed upon the Iser.

'When he offered me Benatek the Emperor called it a castle,' Tycho Brahe said; 'it is hardly that. I am making extensive alterations and enlargements, but one can only do so much, one is frustrated at every turn. His majesty is sympathetic, but he cannot attend in person to every detail. The manager of the crown estates, with whom I must chiefly deal, is not so well disposed toward me as I might wish. Mühlstein he is called, Kaspar von Mühlstein.' Darkly he measured the name, as a hangman would a neck. 'I think he is a Jew.'

It was past noon, but apparently the Dane was breakfasting, for a servant entered now bearing hot bread wrapped in napkins, and a jug from which he filled their cups with a steaming blackish stuff. Kepler peered at it, and Tycho said: 'You do not know this brew? It comes from Araby. I find it sharpens the brain wonderfully.' It was nonchalantly said, yet Kepler understood well enough that he was meant to be impressed by these grand sybaritic things he was being permitted to sample. He drank, and pursed his lips appreciatively, and Tycho, for the first time, smiled. 'You must forgive me, Herr Kepler, that I did not come myself to greet you on your arrival. As I mentioned in my letter, I seldom go to Prague, unless it is to call upon the Emperor; and besides, the opposition at this time of Mars and Jupiter, as you will appreciate, encouraged me not to interrupt my work. However, I trust you will understand that I receive you now less as a guest than as a friend and colleague.'

This address, despite the seeming warmth of the words, left them both obscurely dissatisfied. Tycho, about to speak again, instead looked sulkily away, to the window and the winter day outside. The servant knelt before the huge tiled stove, feeding pine logs to the flames. A youngish fellow, he had a cropped head and meaty hands and raw red feet stuck into wooden clogs. Kepler sighed; he was, he realised, hopelessly of that class which notices the state of servant's feet. He drank some more of the Arabian brew. It did clear the head, but it seemed also, alarmingly, to be giving him the shakes. He feared that his fever was coming on again. It had dogged him now for six months and more, and led him, especially in grey dawn hours, to believe he was consumptive. Still, he seemed to be putting on fat: this cursed ruff was choking him.

'If I might—' he began, but got no farther, for Tycho Brahe turned again and, looking at him hard, asked: 'You work the metals?'

'Metals?' said Kepler faintly. The Dane had produced a small lacquered ointment box, and was applying a dab of aromatic salve to the flesh surrounding the false bridge of silver and gold alloy set into his damaged nose —he had as a young man been disfigured in a duel. Kepler wondered confusedly if this talk of metals meant that he was to be asked to fashion perhaps a new and finer organ to adorn the Dane's great face, and he was relieved when Tycho, with a trace of irritation, said:

'I mean the alembic and so forth. You claimed to be a natural philosopher, did you not?' He had an unsettling way of ranging back and forth in his talk, as if the subject were marked on the counters of a game which he was idly playing in his head.

'No no, alchemy is not, I am not—'

'But you make horoscopes.'

'Yes, that is when I—'

'For payment?'

'Well, yes.' He had begun to stammer. He felt he was being forced to confess to an essential meanness of character. Shaken, he gathered himself for a counter-attack, but Tycho abruptly shifted the direction of play again, saying:

'Your work is of great interest. I have read the *Mysterium cosmographicum* with attention. I did not agree with your conclusions, of course, but your methods I find significant.'

Kepler swallowed. 'You are too kind.'

'Not at all. The flaw, I would suggest, is that you have based your theories upon the Copernican system.'

Instead of on *yours*, that is. Well, at least they were touching on the real matter now. Kepler, with his fists clenched in his lap to stop their trembling, sought feverishly for the best means of proceeding at once to the essential question. However, he found himself, to his annoyance, hesitating. He did not trust Tycho Brahe. The man was altogether too still and circumspect, like a species of large lazy predator hunting motionless from the sprung trap of his lair. (Yet he was, in his way, a great scientist. That was some reassurance. Kepler believed in the brotherhood of science.) And besides, what *was* the essential question? Modest though he imagined his needs to be, he was seeking more than mere accommodation for himself and his family at Benatek. Life to him was a kind of miraculous being in itself, a living organism almost, of wonderful complexity and grace, wracked, though, by a chronic wasting fever; he wished from Benatek and its master the granting of a perfect order and quietude in which he might learn to contain his life, to still its fevered thrashings and set it to dancing the grave dance. Now, as he brooded in some dismay on these confusions, the moment eluded him. Tycho, pushing away the picked bones of his breakfast, began to rise. 'Shall we see you at dinner, Herr Kepler?'

'But—' The astronomer was scrabbling after his hat.

'You will meet some other of my assistants then, and we can discuss a redistribution of tasks, now that we are one more. I had thought of setting you the lunar orbit. However, we must first consult my man Longomontanus, who has a say in these matters, as you will of course understand.' They made a slow exit from the room. Tycho did not so much walk as cruise, a stately ship. Kepler, pale, twisted the hatbrim in his trembling fingers. This was all mad—he was being treated as nothing more than a laboratory assistant! Yet even in the midst of his dismay he could not fail to acknowledge the comedy of the situation. The spectacle of his affairs coming asunder, as they seemed always doomed to do, like mad machines, provoked in an obscure crevice of his mind a helpless annihilating laughter, too secret and unruly to be allowed to register in his face as anything more than a tense twitching of eyelid and lip. In the corridor Tycho Brahe bade him an absent-minded farewell, and cruised away. In the cavernous guest rooms Frau Barbara awaited him. She had an air always of seeming cruelly neglected, by his presence no less than by his absence. Sorrowing and expectant, she asked:

'Well?'

Kepler selected a look of smiling abstraction and tested it gingerly. 'Humm?'

'Well,' his wife insisted, 'what *happened?*'

'O, we had breakfast. Or he had breakfast, while I had, I suppose, lunch. See, I brought you something,' and produced from its hiding place in the crown of Baron Hoffman's hat, with a conjuror's flourish, an orange. 'And I had coffee!'

Regina, who had been leaning out at the open window, turned now and advanced upon her stepfather with a faint, somehow solemn and, it seemed, sympathetic smile. She was a strange child. Under her candid gaze he felt always a little shy.

'There is a dead deer in the courtyard,' she said. 'If you lean out far you can see it, on a cart. It's very big.'

'That is an elk,' said Kepler gently. 'It's called an elk. It got drunk, you know, and fell down stairs when—'

Their baggage had come up, and Barbara had been unpacking. With the glowing fruit cupped in her hands she sat down suddenly amidst the strewn wreckage of their belongings and began to weep. Kepler and the child stared at her.

'You settled nothing!' she wailed. 'You didn't even *try.*'

DERMOT HEALY

A Family and a Future

I NEVER SAW THEM GO OUT that way in their cars by night. The new Ford Consuls, perhaps a Morris Minor, Volkswagons, were always popular round that recalcitrant time. I can only imagine the secrets the night holds, the vulnerability of the isolated sex-object, the daring curiosity of those frightened, frustrated men and always the rumours of decadent tragedy. Perhaps those frightened, sharp-suited men would be walking up the road throwing nervous glances to the left and right of them. Or more assuredly, I'd say, in the heat of drink and summer they would drive bravely out to that beautiful place, where the Erne breaks sparklingly asunder between the forests, play the horn going past the cottage and collect her at her innocent, prearranged places.

For this is real pornography, to imagine the habits of June rather than describe them with authenticity, those quick flitting affairs where Oughter thundered. Or the beat of visionary passion across an ancient cemetery overrun with shadows, for illicit lovers have always favoured as their first jousting place the quiet of the grave.

June was three years older than myself. She lived with an ailing though resilient mother, cantankerous, shoddy, quick-witted from dealing aggressively with shy people and successful farmers, June's father had been carried off by a fever from drinking contaminated water. Thus she took on the feeding of the few cattle that remained, carrying buckets of water from a spring well a mile away, dousing her socks, since the nearby well had never been cleared up or limestoned after the poisoning. She looked after the chopping of timber from the multitudinous forest of the Lord, facilitated dispassionately and excitedly the emissions of her neighbourly brethren.

From the locality she extended her doings to the town.

What had been mere sensual caprice, became decadent business overnight.

I never then saw her in a pub or encountered her on the way to the Cathedral.

Befitting a hard worker, her body was strong but fat. She was not in the least goodlooking. But, because of the dark lashes, June's brown eyes confirmed that traditional estimation of beauty by the Gaelic bards of the area. . . . You, the highest nut in the place. Tanned from wandering the fields after lost cattle she would wander through the market on fair day, watched by the treacherous eyes of the stall-holders, in ribbons and patched skirt, huge hips akimbo. The Louis heels of her pink shoes worn sideways because of the edge of her walk, dots of mud on the back of her seamed nylons. The street-corner folk would hail her as she passed. She might loiter by the winter Amusements, a little astray among the jargon of lights and fortune-telling, in those days when the giddy voice of Buddy Holly filled the side-streets with 'I guess it doesn't matter any more'. But she was always attracted to the rifle range. Cold-blooded curses helped her aim. Her brown eyes squinted down and steadied on the centre of life, on the yellow thin heart of a crow, on the marked cap of a jester.

I was never attracted to her but we always spoke. Like Hallo, and How is the crack, and How is it going.

But I did see her father's polka-dotted tie that held up her worn knickers.

I was sick, about thirteen and on the back of a bike travelling along the edge of the railway lines. Sweeney dropped the bike when he saw June chasing a Red Devon cow across a field, from East to West, and the two of them fell together among the coltsfoot and daffodils, stripped in the frost and she masturbated him and then me, and there was something virulent about his satisfaction, something slow and remorselessly painful about mine.

It was her desire and detachment, my desire of love. And then Sweeney mounted her some time later and she called to him, for a minute stop, stop, you're hurting, but he didn't and then she fainted. Her brown face keeled over in the frost, her father's tie round her ankles, and a look of horrified petulance on his face, stood under a leafless oak, his brown cock unbloodied but fading. He would I think have buried her there had she not come to. But what did I say or do in those moments? Nursed her head in my lap, called to her, sung to her? Was I not at that moment as much to blame for her misfortune? But Sweeney returned with water and aspirins from a nearby house, she drank as I coaxed her, her eyes swam and steadied and then she thanked us, once more restored, she set off to capture the beast she had been following. And Sweeney shouted after her, I'm sorry June, and many's the time after they were lovers. For years too I was afflicted by this scene, in my dream I would too be about to come, and try to restrain for fear of hurting her, wake painfully in the dark, sperm like acid on my thighs. No, she never went into a pub for she never reached the peak of adult debauchery. Hers will always be the brink, the joyous, disparate moments of adolescence. Till none of the country folk bothered her, till she became the shag, the ride, the jaunt of the town. Eventually the police took a hand and barred her from the precincts, from her nocturnal clambering into parked buses at the depot, doors opened by skilled mechanics, from stretching under an impatient, married man in the waiting room of the railway station. Thus those cars would be leaving town to pick up June, single or in groups, the hub-bub of careless laughter to spread her juices across the warm leather upholstery.

It was around this time that Benny met her, I think. He had been hired out to a farm in Dundalk for five years previous, and one full lush May he returned for the cancerous death of his last parent. Benny had a red freckled face, wore hunting caps, was a loner. He took her to the pictures, her first normal romance began. She was under great distress, as it was her first time in the cinema and they moved twice till she was immaculately placed one row behind the four-pennies. It was not short-sightedness but enthusiasm. Over his shoulder she stole timorous, enquiring glances at Maureen O'Hara, as the square filled up with wounded soldiers from the Civil War. Benny was to linger on a further three years in Dundalk, but that December he returned again to his deserted house, they cut trees together in the Christmas tree wood and sold them in the snowed-up market place, two shillings apiece, a week before the festival. Pheasants were taken with a shot of blood and feathers from the cloudy skies above Oughter and presented by him to June's house for the seasonal dinner. Which he attended, the wily gossiping stranger, with a bottle of Jameson and orange.

But that was the first Christmas. The second or third he never came. June had mothered a child. By a solicitor, a priest, by myself, does it matter? That summer too her mother made it to the bath in time to vomit up a three-foot tapeworm. The old lady's skin and bone retreated under the shock. The release of the worm and birth of the child occurred within a week of each other. June grew thin again, her mother fattened. They grew more friendly, dependent upon each other. That year too, during these trying times, when they were burning the gorse and the furze, a fire swept the hill behind the house. And the two sick ladies fought the flames, shouting encouragement to each other, retreated successfully, covered in ash, their blouses scorched, their arms thrown around each other, laughing, and stood together that evening holding up the newly washed child to look at the smoking field.

Neighbours came and mended their own fences and kept their counsel to themselves.

The drama of that fiery evening was that it led to a reunion between

Benny and June and the dry-skinned baby. He came and repaired the
scorched sheds, replaced the burnt rafter, renailed the twisted galvanise
and played with the child in the cool kitchen, braved the mad, wandering
talk of the mother. From the window you could see the water breaking
out there like it was hitting water-coloured rocks. Sails skimmed through
the trees, boat engines roared, and behind, a less formidable beauty, en-
dowed darkly and modern among the pines, with wooden seats and toi-
lets for viewing the lake, a black modern cafe with chain-motifs on a
cleared rise.

Soon the tourists would be arriving. 'To paint a dark corner darker'
the old lady said. 'Think of who sired him that built yon'. She held the
bowl of soup at arm's length, licking her wrists and fists, grey brown-
tinged hair, deep-blue flowered nightcoat, fluffy shoes, yellow nightdress
peeking out at her strained neck, awkward movements. 'The architect,
the gobshite, came in here to explain, all airs and graces. Then he started
a fucking dirge. We told him where to get off'.

June was on the grass, on all fours, scrambling away from the child
and Benny smoked by the window.

They married, herself and Benny, the following April. And the next
time I saw them was at a dance at the opening of that cafe, where as yet
only light drinks were being served, given by the local G.A.A. I was mes-
merized after a day's drinking, and in drunken fashion attended to their
every need, needing heroes myself but at some point I got into an argu-
ment and was set upon by a couple of bastards from the town. They
ripped at my face with fingers like spurs, broken glasses tore at my
throat. I heard the hand breaking down, heels grated against my teeth.
Lying there babbling and crying on the floor while the fight went on over
my head. June came and hauled me free and Benny swung out left, right
and centre. They caught Benny's eye a fearful blow and all I can remember then is an Indian doctor in the hospital complaining of having had
enough of attending to drunks in the middle of the night. But a nurse
stitched my scalp back onto my head and my head back onto my body.

As for Benny, he was taken away to the Eye and Ear hospital in Dublin
where he was ably attended to and where I called on him. We shared few
words, because only fighting brought out the intimacy in us. My life then
for a number of years was spent in aggravating silly details. Benny returned to Dundalk to complete a final year and June took on other lovers, she mothered another child. With his money saved Benny returned a
year later in Spring for good. Shrunken reeds had washed up, carquet,
light brown, two ducks flying together, the dark blowing in. Cars were
parked on the entrance to the cafe, which was now a magnificent hotel,
with C & W stickers on them. The little Pleasure House of the Lord of the
Estate had been renewed by the Minister of Lands with new bright pebble

dash, and renamed. Going up a new lane seemed miles, coming back mere yards.

I was out at the Point after an endless day's fishing, without a catch, curlews screaming in the background, cormorants fanning themselves in heraldic postures at the top of the castle. Benny and I stood together chatting. But aloof too from each other, for things change; sometimes you are only an observer, at other times you are involved intimately in other people's lives, but now as a mere recorder of events and personages, the shock of alienation arrived on me, yet deeper than that the ultimate intimacy of disparate lives.

Benny said that June's house was a well-seasoned, weathered cottage. His own deserted one had grown accustomed to rats, the dead people that had lived in the house, his parents, could often be heard arguing at night by passersby. He only went up there by daylight to fodder the cattle. The hum of taped music drifted down from the hotel.

They have everything at their fingertips above, he said pointing. Take your money boy from whatever angle it's coming from.

He pulled out his pipe and knocked it off a stone. A cormorant flew by, its coarse black wings aflutter, beak like silver in the spring sun, that set now without the lake catching its reflection. For it was far West of the pines. Some people neglect their experiences by holding them at arm's length, at verbal distancing. Not so Benny, his generosity of spirit was personal, abrupt. Behind us, June's three kids were playing, only one of whom I think resembled him. They were all beautifully turned out, like out of a bandbox, not a hair out of place. The eldest had straight black hair, gypsy-like, and seemed to reflect humourously on things. The youngest had fair curly locks, talked of TV programmes, wide astonished eyes, blue. The four-year old had undistinguished auburn hair, colourless skin. She stood between us, intent upon the fishing and saying and interrupting all the beautiful encouraging things for life that a child can tell or repel.

The waves were heavy and cold as rock. Feeling was dispersed by the heart, intestines and lungs. Like embryos, sluggishly drops of water broke away from under the ice and flowed, ice-covered. He, Benny, didn't turn round to look at the cars as I did. He gossiped away, cruel, erratic, interested in the beyond. As if he knew the laundered space of each guilty psyche, and how each family renews itself for the future. For though, over the past few months, myself and Benny may have dispensed with familiarity, except for the cheerful courtesies, all's well. For you see they had his house scourged for years, those amiable frightened men, but now seemingly all's settled. June has given him joy and sustenance, and she maintains an aura of doubtful reserve, and I don't see her any more.

FRANK ORMSBY

Interim

Five years ago we knew such ecstasies
As who in half-dead countrysides find strong
The least life stirring;
We sang first lines and thought we had learned the song.

Six months of marriage sobered us. We found,
Not disenchantment, more a compromise
Charged with affection.
We settled to the limited surprise

That day-to-day insists on, brought to bear
A fact to manage by, a quiet light
That gave its own warmth,
And knew our walking grown to sudden flight

When least expected. O, I loved those years
Of unforced loving, when the urge to stray
Was lulled to sleeping,
And hearth and kitchen sink were nothing grey.

Now, once again, I notice carefree girls
In streets, on buses. Tied, I can't but see
Their untried promise,
All the lost futures catching up with me.

The nerve to be unfaithful is the lack
That curbs my yearnings. Soon again I'm sure,
And pleased to be,
Of trusting wife, my own furniture.

What binds us, love? I struggle to define
Its shifting substance. What strange seeds are met
Within us, fashion there in our despite
This hybrid, half-contentment, half-regret?

Tonight, uncertain if the dreams have cracked,
Let's seek behind the possible illusions
How much is gone, how much remains intact;
Let's talk of change and come to no conclusions.

A Small Town in Ireland

The roads run into it and out.
   About the bridge the people go.
Someone was executed there,
   (Was it two hundred years ago?)

Is sung of still. But I would sing
   A roof, a door, a set of bricks,
Because you entered Ireland there
   One night in nineteen forty-six.

These are the rails your fingers touched
   Passing to school, the waves below
You dipped your toes in. That is all
   The history I would want to know,

Were not the waters those that eyes
   Had flung their final glance upon,
Coursing, untouched and blameless, past the loss
   Of someone's lover, someone's son.

A Country Cottage: Towards Dawn

We turned before we reached it, the sky-pressed tiles,
The squat walls drowning in discoloured light,
The windows glazed with morning.
Far off a helicopter was troubling the dawn,
Hills braced themselves against the reckless clouds.

You told me how a son went missing there
Some months before, of office-workers' hands
In stranded seaweed and a line of men
Searching the drains and culverts.
A doctor found his body in the reeds of a cold lough.

So tense the hour an ear would not divine
Our speech as love, our trailing steps as lovers'
Stretching the minutes. If eyes were opening there
They could not know the thing we wished them
From the road's shadow or find much comfort in it

And so we turned.
Behind the yard was bristling with the dead
Warnings not even day could counter now:
When cars creep in the lay-by, bar the gate,
When feet press on the gravel, turn the key.

CIARAN CARSON

The Insular Celts

Having left solid ground behind
In the hardness of their place-names,
They have sailed out for an island:

As along the top of a wood
Their boats have crossed the green ridges,
So has the pale sky overhead

Appeared as a milky surface,
A white plain where the speckled fish
Drift in lamb-white clouds of fleece.

They will come back to the warm earth
And call it by possessive names—
Thorned rose, love, woman and mother;

To hard hills of stone they will give
The words for breast; to meadowland,
The soft gutturals of rivers,

Tongues of water; to firm plains, flesh,
As one day we will discover
Their way of living, in their death.

They entered their cold beds of soil
Not as graves, for this was the land
That they had fought for, loved, and killed

Each other for. They'd arrive again:
Death could be no horizon
But the shoreline of their island,

A coming and going, as flood
Comes after ebb. In the spirals
Of their brooches is seen the flight

Of one thing into the other:
As the wheel-ruts on a battle-
Plain have filled with silver water,

The confused circles of their wars,
Their cattle-raids, have worked themselves
To a laced pattern of old scars.

But their death, since it is no real
Death, will happen over again
And again, their bones will seem still

To fall in the hail beneath hooves
Of horses, their limbs will drift down
As the branches that trees have loosed.

We cannot yet say why or how
They could not take things as they were.
Some day we will learn of how

Their bronze swords took the shape of leaves,
How their gold spears are found in cornfields,
Their arrows are found in trees.

The Half-Moon Lake

It was here the boy entered the skylight
And was gone, into the reversed world
Of his dreams, hoping that life there might

Prove otherwise. Walking the tentative
Pane of ice there might have been that morning,
He would have imagined himself to live

In one final image, the star-shaped hole
Approaching darkly, sudden as his
Disappearance from our lives. Or had his soul

Just then been frailed too taut
For human heart, had the white sheet
Already failed beneath him at the thought?

No-one heard him go in silence,
Nor when they dragged for him, deep as chance
Allowed, was there any trace.

Was the faultless mirror shattered
By the thin boy diving for the moon
Of his own face rising through the water?

They could not yet say why
He left so quickly, not leaving any word,
Or whether the glass existed purely

For his own forgetfulness. Deep
In the unseen water it is possible
He lies, with himself at last asleep.

It was for the other children that they feared.
It had been necessary that the Half-Moon Lake be
Filled in, and altogether disappear.

Soot

It was autumn. First, she shrouded
The furniture, then rolled back the carpet
As if for dancing; then moved
The ornaments from the mantelpiece,
Afraid his roughness might disturb
Their staid fragility.

He came; shyly, she let him in,
Feeling ill-at-ease in the newly-spacious
Room, her footsteps sounding hollow
On the boards. She watched him kneel
Before the hearth, and said something
About the weather. He did not answer,

Too busy with his work for speech.
The stem of yellow cane creaked upwards
Tentatively. After a while, he asked
Her to go outside and look, and there,
Above the roof, she saw the frayed sunflower
Bloom triumphantly. She came back

And asked how much she owed him, grimacing
As she put the money in his soiled hand.
When he had gone, a weightless hush
Lingered in the house for days. Slowly,
It settled; the fire burned cleanly;
Everything was spotless.

Hearing that soot was good for the soil,
She threw it on the flowerbeds. She would watch
It crumble, dissolving in the rain,
Finding its way to lightless crevices,
Sleeping, till in spring it would emerge softly
As the ink-bruise in the pansy's heart.

NEIL JORDAN

Fragment from a Novel in Progress

I HAVE TO IMAGINE you Rene since he took no photographs. She did, but only after he had died. This conspiracy of white and silence. In the convent on Sion Hill Road, to which you went five months later than you should have. You have a broad face for a child, eyes that could be seen as too small, but who cared. Not much of the beauty so many would claim for you later, but that was always contradicted too, with phrases like What's all the fuss about, She's no oil-painting, Nothing extraordinary. Not much either of that non-physical quality for which so many words would be culled, words like Innocence, Quiet Charisma, Genius, for living I mean. You were an ordinary child in every respect and what greater blessing can one ask for, than to have an ordinary childhood?

It's just your hair that is distinctive. Curls, hanging all around your forehead. Your hair is thin but has a creaminess of texture that gives each strand its own way of falling. Flat near the crown but falling all around it to a fringe of spirals, like those clumps of flowers the stems of which droop from the centre and the petals fall to make the rim of a bell. Blonde is a shade that catches the tints of the colours around it. Your hair is nearest to that white, being blonde. Your hair is cream blonde and catches most lights and the outer strands make a halo of them. To have extraordinary hair is almost as good a thing as to have an ordinary childhood.

And out of that white and silence. You sat with Lili on the small benches and the Cross and Passion nuns moved among the benches like beings from another world. Their heads were framed by those great serge and linen bonnets and nodded like boxes when they spoke. It is you at the time that Lili described, when your father would walk in in his Free State uniform and lift you onto one hip and then the other, trying to avoid paining you with his shoulder strap or his shoulder pistol while the gun-carriage rattled outside and the nuns whispered like a litany their offers of tea. You would have been near six then. And your clearest memory could have been mine. Of the beech tree in the gravelled yard across from the windows of the classroom. The trunk is huge and intrudes straight out of

189

the earth and the gravel is thick around, revealing no earth or roots to prepare one for its intrusion. It backs in its magnificence against an old granite wall and such is its strength that the branches nearest the wall have been sawed off to stop them crushing through the granite. So all growth of branch and foliage is towards the school, towards the window at which you would have sat, staring. It is really for you, the severed half-umbrella, the monstrous segment of tangled growth that shades half the yard. Across from it again is a small shrubbery, half-bald with grass, smoothed by generations of small feet. A bell would have rung, a fragile shiver of brass notes filling the classroom around you, the nun's bonnet would have nodded towards the door and you and the class would have walked jerkily towards the door and once outside expended yourself in that circular burst of energy that erupts from nowhere and ends nowhere, scouring the gravel with your feet, the air filled with a patina of cries that seems to hover above your heads. Only when you had exhausted yourself would you lie by the tree. But the tree would renew spent energies, would gather a ring of small bodies around it, each newcomer jostling to rest their back against the bark. You would have won Rene, continually won, by reason of that quiet ignorance of the turmoil of others which would always have found its few square feet of bark. The bark moulded in scallops, rougher than skin is.

Your name would have brought you some attention among the Eileens, Maureens, Marys and Brids. Two thin white vowels, strangely unIrish and yet so easily pronounced, as if more Irish than the Irish names. Your father's visits would have brought you more. Most of the nuns would have baulked at the excesses of the troubles but would have supported the Free State side and have been overcome by the mystique of your father's name. He looks a little like a statue, standing in the doorway. Two of them though would have refused to be impressed. One from Clare, with Republican connections whose tight mouth whenever she passèd you in the corridor would have said enough. And one old, quite beautiful creature, an avid reader of Tolstoy who would have regarded the presence of gun-carriages in a school yard as an immoral intrusion. She is old and tall, like a long translucent insect underneath her habit. The thin bones on her hands and the shining white skin on them and her cheeks, which is all you can see of her beneath the black, seem to contain more reserves of energy than any of the younger novices. Her hands are hardly warm, they hardly linger on your hair for more than a moment, each of her movements is as brief as it can possibly be as if her body is reserving itself for a boundless, ultimate movement. And the reserve, the iron quiet that she has imposed on her life has had its recompense in the cheeks that face you at the top of the class, as smooth and pallid as those of a young, inactive boy, in the grey eyes under the black and white bonnet which reflect the impersonal rewards of a lifetime's confinement. Her presence is hypnotic, as are her maxims. 'Keep your hands', she tells you, 'to yourself. Keep your hands from yourself'. You cannot understand the contradictions of this dictate, but through your efforts to understand them it assumes a sense of truth that is, for you, greater than words. It hints at the mystery behind movement and gesture. You say the maxim to yourself in situations that have nothing to do with hands. You know the ideal is hands folded and demure on the lap of your folded legs, neither to nor from yourself and you know too that this is not the final answer which, you suspect, has nothing to do with the dimpled, fleshly hands before you. Are there other hands, you wonder, unseen ones which these real hands must train to lie at rest, ready to suddenly bloom into a gesture of giving? The hands of the soul, you think and stare at the nun who has repeated her maxim once more and is sitting, hands unseen, at the top of the class-room. Her name is Sister Michael and it expresses that maleness which must be the ultimate goal of her sisterhood.

Lili is your seat-mate. She is pert and alive, master of the social graces of that classroom. If anyone is the favourite it is she, catching the glances of nuns with the downward flickering of her eyelids. And even now I can see the small alert girl who would have arbitrated the loves and hatreds of that class, whose clothes would have been imitated, cut of hair, colour of ribbon, style of bow. She had a silver tooth-brace even then which gave her a lisp and the lisp becomes in her an enviable possession. She is en-thralled by you and your cream-blonde hair and yet can dominate you with her quickness and her tongue, for yours was more than anything an ordinary childhood.

You sit by the window and stare at the trunk of the beech. Sister Mi-chael's voice wavers, like a thread held in air. Lili, to see the trunk, has to lean past you. You watch the shadow of its severed umbrella blacken less and less of the yard as the morning progresses. The first break passes and the second break till the final bell rings and you run in the yard once more and find your space against the bark and if the armoured carrier is there, you are carried off in that and if it isn't, begin the long walk down the Trimelston Road home.

The wind sweeps down the long avenue at one end of which there is a half-built church with a new kind of granite and cement which make the half-walls rise sheer and inhuman. How large it will be and what a God it will hold. There is a group of boys playing near nettles chanting 'up Dev'. One of them is standing in the nettles, crying and leaping to retrieve his cap which either the wind or the other boys have flung. You stagger with Lili through the wind, it is a spring wind and pulls the green of all the sycamores in the one way, towards the sea. There is the line of coast houses behind you and the sea, which seems hardly disturbed. You walk a few steps and turn to the sea and then face the wind again and walk. Lili is laughing and clutching her gym-slip. The wind makes another sweep, you close your eyes against it and a melody suddenly courses through you like a long pendulum sweeping the tips of the sycamores in a heavenly arc. It runs its course and finishes and just when it seems past recall it comes again, its long brass tones fortified by another one and you listen and walk while the two melodies boom through you. There is a rhythm of which each tree seems a distinct beat and the bass song, too deep for any human voice. It recurs and recurs with each sweep of the wind which pulls your slip against you, gripping your knees and thighs as if it were wet. Your limbs are almost too small to bear it but you know you have to listen to that awesome pressure of beauty though your body and your years might sigh with relief each time it goes. When it leaves you finally and the wind dies down you are relieved. You turn once more to the coast houses and the unruffled line of blue and then walk on with Lili, not saying a word. The boy has retrieved his cap and is standing near the nettles, smearing his legs with dock-leaves, crying softly. Lili stops, looks at him as if she might console him, but then walks on. 'Cry-babby!' she whispers.

You walk past him, looking at his green-smeared knees. You have little that is defined or personal about you. You have not yet reached the age of reason. The melody flies and your soul waits for its return. You are like a mirror that catches other people's breath. One nun refers to you as that plump, blonde-haired girl, another talks of your slender, almost nervous quietness. You willingly become each, as if answering the demands every gaze makes on you. The most persistent attitude towards you is one of pity, touched by a warm, moral, faintly patriotic glow. You are the child whose father must rarely see her, immersed as he is in the affairs of the Free State, whose mother perhaps sees her even less. Through you they see your heritage, the glow of newsprint and newspaper reports, the profusion of rumours and heated discussions beside which you must seem something of an afterthought. You grow, through the very stuff of those frustrated politics. You are Lili's most treasured possession, the prize that all her classroom graces have won her. Though you are most at ease when unnoticed.

Are you already choosing between these alternatives as to which of them you will eventually become? A choice that must be unconscious, but within which must lie the birth of real decision, as those glances we throw as a child are the breeding-ground for the tone of gaze as an adult. Or are you, behind the screen of your ordinary childhood, holding each of them in balance, nurturing each to take part in the eventual you? For you did become all of them. You hold your hands folded, a modest distance from your body on the classroom desk. Your knuckles are still only dimples, but from those particular dimples a particular knuckle will eventually emerge. Walking down the Trimelston Road the sea is always in front of you, a broad flat ribbon at first and then, as the road falls, a thinner strip of blue serge till eventually, when the coast houses rise to your eyes, it finds itself a thin, irregular grey thread.

One day there is a statue in the window with the year's first daffodils arranged around it in jamjars, half-full of water. The statue seems frozen in an attitude of giving. The silver nun teaches you the austere beauty of its observance, tells you that this is the first of May, the beginning of Summer, Mary's month. And all those girls, more than half the class, whose first name is Mary or some gaelicisation of it, Maureen, Maire, Mairead, bow their heads and smile.

You look at the thin yellow daffodils flapping in their jamjars on the sill of the window behind which the beech tree can be seen studded with green now as if the month of May had hastily flecked it with a stiff green paintbrush. You can hardly isolate any one spot of green from the tentative mass but you still try, with your young girl's eyes, their imperfection of focus, their totality of concentration. The points which are in fact small buds and which in Autumn will become broader leaves with the texture of beech nuts and bark resist all your attempts to isolate them, merge and separate and finally through the tiredness of your eyes become what seems to be a pulsating mist, forming a halo the limits of which you can't define around that unlikely trunk, much like your own hair, which you also must be able to see reflected in the window-glass and the image of your own blonde halo becomes merged with first green pulsating of the month of May. You look from the confusion of yellow, blonde and green to the black and white frame of Sister Michael's face who is explaining in her silver voice the intricacies of May devotions. How the name was filtered through to light on half the female populace of this small nation, the class. You cannot know that your first name should have been Brigit, Mary of the Gael. Sister Michael tells you that the class will replace those flowers daily.

The narcissism which allows you confuse the glowing strands of hair round your face with the mass of half-formed leaves on the beech-tree, the yellow bells of the daffodils is an innocent one and more than that, an honest one, and perhaps even more than that, a happy one, an unlooked-for gift that in later life will be the one thing friends will agree that is yours, that must have shown its first contours in childhood. Later that night your nurse bathes you. Her name is May, she must have minded you since your mother's nights were divided between performance, rehearsal and political meeting. She takes you into your mother's room to dry yourself, wrapped in a towel, to the centre of that soft carpet, surrounded by the mirrors of that open wardrobe, the dressing-table and the oval, quite mysterious mirror on the wash-table with its enamel basin and swollen jug. The towel is draped around you as May massages your hair. Then your neck and your shoulders, and it gradually slips down as she rubs your stomach, your calves and your small feet till you can see yourself, naked and dry in the three mirrors. Your stare has the concentration of a dream. Your body is all dimples, the dimples of your breasts, your navel, your vagina, knuckles and knees. These dimples will in fact grow like the pinpoints of green round the umbrella of beech, way beyond Mary's month into the shapes of womanhood and you suspect this and your suspicion has the texture and emotional presence of the colours green, blonde and yellow that filled you earlier, but if it is a colour its hue is unearthly since you cannot picture it, merely feel it in the emotional centre where colours move you. May leaves the room to get your clothes. You are most attracted towards the mirror that is out of your reach, the oval one above the washbasin. You drag over a chair and stand on it and try to see your flesh behind the reflections of the swollen jug and the basin. Your look is scientific in its innocence. You lean forward to see yourself better behind the white curves of the jug but you can't and so you stare into the water in the basin. You are reflected there, from above. Your face looms over your own cream expanse, shimmering in the water, your blonde curls sticking to your crown. You hear a gasp behind you and turn to see May aghast in the doorway. The chair totters and you fall, bringing basin jug and water with you. You land in the wet pool and your elbow scrapes off the enamel curve and spurts blood. It runs down your belly and thighs, turning pink with the water. May runs forward with a stream of prayers and admonitions and grabs a towel and wrings it in the water and wipes your thighs and wrings it again. She blesses herself with her other hand.

It must be soon after this that you reach the age of Reason which like the age of the earlier maxims makes the undifferentiated flow of your experience manifest and outward, placing it neatly in language and time, allowing others to say to you that you are different now from what you were then. And though you wonder how such a change could creep on you unawares yet when you hear Sister Michael explain the metaphysics of Reason to the class (though she seems to be speaking only to you) you accept that you must be different if only because you are being told so, you accept that your days and memories up to this moment are one thing and after that moment will be another. You suspect a cruelty behind this knowledge though and wonder whether if you hadn't been given it would the same be true. She tells you how up to that moment you could not sin because you were not aware of sin but how after that moment the awareness of sin that she is handing you like a gift will make it possible for you to sin. And you accept a further slice of knowledge which defines this sense of difference in you, the fact that now every action will have to be balanced and passed between the twin primaries of sin and virtue, and that between them there will be an expanse of medial tones and that yet no matter how fragile this difference in tone there will always come a point where white swings imperceptibly into black and beyond which you will be able to say, Now I have sinned. You wonder whether this sense of sin is a gift to be developed, whether you must learn to sin as you once learnt to walk. You sense that these words she is imposing on the flow of your days are somewhat arbitrary, like the words she underlines, for obscure reasons, on the hymns she chalks on the blackboard. And yet there is comfort in the language and Sister Michael has after all impressed on you that knowledge can never be useless. You toy with this new knowledge, imagining some use for it while Sister Michael continues with an image of the soul as a droplet of pure water coming from God (and you imagine God then to be a sea, remembering the water that splashed you from the falling basin, for a droplet must come from some larger expanse and a sea is the largest expanse you can imagine; but since a droplet always comes from above and the sea is always below you suspect that this sea must not be the sea you know, always the lowest point in the landscape, but a sea that is placed somewhere above your experience, mirroring the sea that you know, permeating you with its backwards waves) into the world, tarnished only by the fact of its birth. But, Sister Michael continues, as our days multiply and as we progress from the age of Innocence to the age of Reason (and here she pauses, implying a multitude of ages, the texture of which you cannot imagine) this droplet becomes tarnished by the grains of hours and the ink of experience and only our own efforts can wash it back to something like its original purity. And you accept this image but fortify it with your own one, of that Ocean in reverse washing over every hour of your days. And there is a slanting pencil of light coming through the window, falling on your hands, which are to yourself and from yourself, shaking slightly because of the wind on the umbrella of buds outside, because between your hands and the sunlight there is the tree. And Sister Michael has continued to describe to you the sacraments that belong to the age of Reason, those of Confession and Communion. She asks you to rehearse the reality. Each of you is to confess to her deskmate the actions which, in the light of Reason, can be seen to be sinful. Lili confesses to you a series of misdemeanours but the air of secrecy and confidence generated by your bowed heads is such that she ends with the confession that she loves you. And you confess to her another series and end with the confession that you love her. And thus you suspect a mystery in Reason, sin and in the droplet of water far more bountiful than that which Sister Michael has explained. Though watching her distribute the tiny pieces of wafer which are to substitute for communion bread you suspect she knows more than she has explained. And feeling Lili's hand curl round yours on the wooden desk you sense that Reason, far from having tarnished your droplet of water, has washed it even purer and even more, has magnified it to a point beyond which it can no longer be considered a droplet, for such is the feeling welling inside you, you suspect it would fill a whole glass. All the other details of the age of Reason seem ancillary to this. The act of Contrition which Sister Michael writes on the blackboard; the pennies of bread which she distributes, which you place on Lili's tongue and she places on yours. And when the big day comes and you wear your white dress that comes nowhere near the brilliance of the yellow daffodils, when the events you have rehearsed take place, your real confession seems to you a pale imitation of your first, rehearsed one. And perhaps you realise that the form of our public acts is only a shadow of that of our private ones, that their landscapes are just reflections and like that real sea below that imaginary sea, with its piers and palms and beaches, reflections in reverse.

It's soon after that that your father collects you, dressed in civvies for once, in a tweed suit and a hat like any middle-class man, a reticent figure in the doorway whom the nuns don't recognise, whose daughter runs to him, whom he holds on his hip in the old way on which she can sit comfortably for once. He carries her through the school to the yard, her blonde hair almost matching the white flecks in his tweed and there's a car there, a young soldier at the wheel. You notice the soldier's ridiculously large cap, you stretch out and tilt it to one side. He doesn't react so you stretch out your hand again but your father stops you, lifts you over the door and places you in the front seat. Then he opens the door and steps in himself, sits you on his knee. The canvas roof of the car is rolled back. The young man drives, but instead of turning right, towards home, he follows the coast road, past the tall houses of Monkstown, through the sedate sea-walks of Kingstown, up towards Killiney and the large mansions with their shutters barred. Your father says little on the drive. He asks you what you did at school and like most children, you tell him nothing. There is a slight pressure from his large hand round your waist which increases as you enter the wide sweep of the Vico Road, which he remembers from the train he took with his year-old wife and his three-month daughter, the Italianite sweep of which told him, more than all the brown fields and woodlands, that he was home. He holds his daughter closer as the blanket of sea disappears among hedges. Her limbs have filled out and her eyes stare up at him with a knowing that is independent of him but that must have come from him and he slowly realises as the car speeds towards Bray that she has grown, between himself and the woman he rarely sees now, miraculously filling the absence between them, garnering her own life from the chaos between theirs and that chaos he sees now must be hopeful and the suspicion rears in his mind again with an elusive truth, with perhaps the last truth, the suspicion in Hyde Park, in the London railway hotels, in the figure of Casement being escorted from the club between a phalanx of policemen that the events which would take hold of him, whose pattern he thought he had divined at the time were weaving quite a different pattern, that the great hatred and passions, the stuff of politics and the movements of men were leading him merely to this child on his jaded knee and that without this child on his knee those movements would have been nothing and would not, he almost suspects, have taken place. This is Bray, he tells her, you have been here before, and she accepts this information and stares, as the driver turns left off Main Street, at the promenade. There is a tiled walk and a railings to one side and below the railings, a beach. There is a line of hotels to the right with a striped canvas canopy over each porch. He motions the car to a halt and tells the driver, whom he calls Jack, to wait. He takes his daughter's hand and walks along the prom and the clasp of their hands is tight and warm as if they both feel, in their different ways, at home. He leads her to an ice-cream stand outside of which there is a board, arrayed with postcards for sale, each postcard bearing a picture of the sea front. She shakes her head when offered an ice-cream, her appetite was never large and so they walk on, her hand bouncing off the railings as if trying to grasp the beach. He misses the canvas huts lining the sea's edge but realises they are out of fashion now, their usefulness outlived since the stray bathers are undressing in full view of the promenade. He considers the same question as he walks, remembering the sweetness of his bathing hut, of the woman to whom he has long stopped sending postal orders. He wonders which is the greater event, his encounter with her or the war of that year, this walk along the promenade or the Treaty bother. They have reached a line of sad Edwardian façades which sweep from the town to make a right-angle with the prom and on the patch of green in front there is an old man painting. Rene stands behind the man and stares at his dabbing brush. He stands behind Rene. He can tell even though the picture is half-finished, even though he rarely looks at paintings, that this one won't be good. But the picture still moves him. It is of a shoreline and sea, but not the sea towards which the man is looking, the sea is a brilliant blue, while the real one is dull metal, grey, and it is lit by a dazzling, garish light that could belong to Italy or Greece, but not to Bray. The naive sheen of those colours seems to come from a sea the old man carries with him. He has a shock of white hair, a high stiff collar and a grey-black suit baggy round the knees, that balance between fine cloth and shabbiness which could be termed Bohemian. His concentration on the canvas has a slight pose about it, as if he is conscious of the figure he cuts and of them watching. And sure enough, he turns to them suddenly without halting the dabbing brush and tells them in a gruff, Protestant voice that they are blocking the light. Look by all means, the painter says, but leave me my light.

The beach has finished now and the promenade has tapered into a small stony walk between the hulk of Bray Head and a rocky sealine. They veer from the walk and go up through a field to the terminal point of the cable-cars. Will we go up? he asks her while a yellow car bears down on them, swinging on its metal rope. She nods, as any child would. We went up before, he tells her, climbing up the metal stairs and into the cabin, you, your mother and me. I don't remember, she tells him, settling in beside him. You were asleep, he answers, in a straw basket. The car lurches into motion and bears them up, the wind whistling more as it rises. He points out Greystones, the Sugarloaf, Dublin and the road of her school. She stares at the painter below on the prom. I would like to stay here, she says. But you can't, he tells her, the car must go down. I could fly, she tells him, if I wished hard enough. She stands in the swaying car, her arms stretched out. Maybe you could, he tells her, looking up. And it is there, when the car is at its highest point and the cables begin to sag again that he stands and holds her, he is overcome, he lifts her to his chest and gasps over and over again the same few words. You are my child, he says, the car swaying with them standing, and hers. And you feel yourself lifted, you feel his sharp bristle at your cheek, the trunk of his chest against yours and his words that seem weeping and ageless course through you like that melody and like a child too you are embarrassed, you are even stiff, you feel his rib-cage crushing you and you understand, when you find your cheek wet with what must be his tears, you understand how much of the age of Reason you have reached. And the cable-car lurches to a halt and he lifts you down and stands you on the bare Head, the grass scoured by so many sight-seers and he lifts you again onto his shoulders, your bare legs round his neck and begins to walk downwards. Always, he tells you, love your mother. And you promise you will, looking over his bobbing shoulders at the paddle-boats below.

PAUL MULDOON

Sir Walter

Would it never have occurred
To you that all those blue cows
Might be some kind of omen?
On nights not gifted by a moon
Would this last edge of Ireland
Not look like the end of the world,

You not be content a landlord
In Valentia the rest of your days?
What of all those perfect women?
Or did their redheaded men,
Who were hostile and colourblind

Both, see to it that you adventured
Elsewhere? Your sails unfurled
A plantation deep in the Virginias.
I picture the hands of a seaman
Outstretched to say what they mean
To an Indian. Freckled and veined
As tobacco leaves, and not yet cured.

Uncle Pat

When I had last negotiated
The long lane to his cottage
I was driving that old convertible
I picked up for next to nothing.

But when I was ready to go
Could I get a glimmer from her?
"There's many's a man bought a car
Has had to buy a hill as well."

199

Well he might know.
Did he not tell the time
By the clock from a Model T Ford?
Hadn't he a hill named after him?

For what he kept in his bedroom
Was nothing ordinary,
Gas-masks, a trunk of German bills,
The bits and pieces of an aeroplane

That had blundered into his meadow.
And what stories he told,
How he smuggled a barrel of butter
While running the gauntlet

Of Customs and B Specials both.
The morning of his funeral
The hearse was wider than the hedges
Of the long lane to his cottage,

That I had last negotiated
No more than six weeks earlier,
When he himself rolled up his sleeves
And pushed me down Pat's Hill.

Lord Hawhaw

Into the raw furrow
A man is broadcasting corn
From a makeshift, bulging apron.
His arm goes to and fro

No less sweetly than her arm,
For sweetly his wife goes
Against the run of the girls
In the scatter-brained harem

Of the munitions-factory.
Yet what's not possible

Among such high explosives,
While he Digs for Victory?

How did she come by the extra money?
Is the foreman one of several?
Might she step from her overall
With just so little ceremony

As she's lain on the ottoman
And had him draw the curtain?
Can he be no more certain
Of the blond, blue-eyed Autumn

Than a bomber is of its target?
For the English will yield
Before this corn has yellowed,
Or so one Englishman has argued.

Truce

It begins with one or two soldiers,
And one or two following,
With hampers over their shoulders.
They might be off wildfowling

As they would another Christmas Day,
So gingerly they pick their steps.
No one seems sure of what to do.
All stop when one stops.

A fire gets lit. Some spread
Their greatcoats on the frozen ground.
Polish vodka, fruit and bread
Are broken out and passed around.

The air of an old German song,
The rules of patience, are secrets
They'll share before long.
They draw on their last cigarettes

As weekend lovers, when it's over,
Would get up from their mattresses
To congratulate each other
And exchange names and addresses.

The Goods

A man could buy anything
He ever desired
In Golightly's Emporium,
From a bale of wire

To a bolt of cotton;
An axe, a skillet,
A flitch of bacon
Or a barrel of salt.

Golightly's own daughter
Was up for sale,
Sweeter than spring water
From a cedar pail.

He called one lunch-hour
With only a buck.
She was weighing flour
From a hundredweight sack;

A skein of pemmican,
A crate of pullets,
Squashes, pumpkins,
An armful of pelts.

In Golightly's Emporium,
Though trade was quiet,
There were still some things
You could get on credit.

HARRY CLIFTON

Three Poems

1. Potscraping

In the middle of the day,
The family all present,
The main meal being taken,
Her busiest time was then.

In their own time
They got up from the table.
With each shut door
The inner silence grew.

She got down to residues,
Potscraping, staring
At blackened insides.
The afternoon set in.

2. Good Therapy

Memory is a masterpiece
For the incapacitated,
The housebound, to complete
In their too spare time.

The beauty of it consists
In the inexhaustible scope
For detail, externalising
Inexhaustible afternoons

When there is nothing
To be done; filling in
Time, sandgrain by sandgrain,
Until the long beach ends

And oozing waves have been
Stayed, with a brushstroke,
In the too-clean drawing-room
Where nothing was to be done.

3. White Lard

Solidification of her world.
It affects the feet first;
With the years, it permeates
The spaces around the heart.

Mother Hubbard must toil
For breath, is housebound now,
Her blood kept cool by standing
In one place the whole time,

Her thoughts concentrated
On pouring boiling fats into jars
To whiten and cool before her
Up on the frosted window, where

Each thought weighs the same.

Picaro

Between adventures, the picaro must lie down
On all-night streets where the warped and friendless are,
An indefinable character the master author leaves
Half-inchoate, while framing his social story.

Another night; unmapped dark between day-chapters
Of his ebullient wanderings in and out of character
Enough to queer the fiction—that's his anarchic way;
The carriers of vapid roadlamps leave him cold.

Action and life distracts itself indoors;
The picaro sags on a love-scarred bench like a puppet
With nexus-wires removed, nervelessly discomposed,
Eyeing the fictions ablaze in rooming-house windows.

He's in need of a room away from alarum and clangour,
To create himself anew, in these nights of no situation,
From all he has seen and been; take time out
From round-the-clock traffic emblazoned into his brain.

He's in need of a room who has nowhere to withdraw
From intentions not his own, picaresque contingencies
He must jump naked into, society's bedlamite,
Dying young, peradventure, or penned into sad institutions.

Between adventures, his author asleep or in ruins,
The picaro lies down out of social mind a while,
Nursing his self-sufficiency, numbed as it is,
Blinking in crazy perspective on stories he's out of.

Manichee Women

From the wrong side
Of a certain glass door
They smile, and the man who decides
To take a whore

Gets one of these instead.
Like a child
Expecting punishment, he lets himself be led,
Deliberately beguiled

By the shape of his own guilt
Going before him up the spiral staircase,
Half his silver spilt
At the first landing, to gain the grace

Of a virginal handmaid
Dealing in clean linen
And a door-key; half again to be paid
To the manichaean

Where she lies, commenting on the size
Of his lapsed integrity,
Leaving him stripped of any excuse
Not to feel self-pity.

All the rest is priceless.
Room with one locked door,
Dimensions of private unforgiveness
Rented for half an hour,

Scented with amnesia, rented again
In the name of the original sin,
Old children's pain.
When did it begin

Inhabiting women's flesh and bone
Behind glass, for the man whom time divides
With that unknown?
This is his other side,

Ushered out the door
By smiling women, crying such childish tears
Whatever for,
A man in his middle years

Pausing on a street
Restless with venial crimes,
Adjusting his business suit,
Checking the time.

EDWARD BRAZIL

Earth

HE WATCHED HER hooped above the stove with the tongs in her brown hands, ducking in and then out of where the fire was quickening with sparks, and the smack of driftwood in the early morning. Fine blackberry hair bundled back by a ribbon to a dark hank lying along the spine, the hurried knot of her apron askew and shifting and the old loose dressing gown soughing over her slippers like ghost-whisperings in the quiet kitchen. He saw her bend and shiver and then straighten up, lean and creamy, and go away, leaving the door swinging, the after-smell of her presence spreading in frail spumes through the room when she vanished.

They hadn't spoken. He tried to remember when they last did. When they last sat down in the one place and talked without having to plan words and meanings. It was back somewhere in another season when the place was in different colours from now. Before the fizz of summer and the long silences of autumn, days of copper when he looked out at the weather and knew that he'd offended her. Speech had become a charity, brief reluctant petals of conversation about silly things like turnips and the need for new buckets. Mostly she shuffled on her own about the house, sound of her moving through the dead rooms, easing her troubles with the endless rearrangement of furniture. Busying herself with brass ornaments, rags, and the reek of polish.

When he came down now in the mornings the boiled eggs were there for him on the table, the spud of one already lopped off for testing. And she would have nothing to say. Just cooking, and sweeping ashes into a pile. She was trying to make him feel whatever it was she herself considered he ought to be feeling. Shame or sorrow or general unease, things he couldn't pretend to profess even for her sake. He resented it all, her efforts to convey by brooding that something had been lost between them, thrown away without care like the coins they tossed once years ago into a well in a special place, a dirty well outside a village, their father's purse spilled out on his lap and he rooting for pennies in the silver.

They should both have married and then parted. He knew that now.

He was certain about himself at least, lying awake in the nights, listening to the wind and the endless rattling of leaves and knowing how fatal it had been to drift and let the days slip by in a flurry. The fortnight every year in London gladdened him. But the West End was a temporary deception, a rush of neon, the jangle of amusement, mad traffic charging along bizarre streets. It was always necessary to return and there was a long year between one holiday and the next.

Sometimes when he went down to the harbour in the evening and there was no one there, he would come upon the dry idea of himself, a notion as dowdy as the stained trousers and the boots he wore. A figure of no consequence, staring at empty boats. Then he would recoil, applying himself to whistling some frivolous tune to perfection.

He went outside, the morning blood quivering in him a second time that day, and posted Schubert at the gate. He threatened a hiding if he should dare move and then traipsed away down through the farm, the house diminishing over his shoulder and the sister shrinking within, doing what she was doing. Probably in her room dusting statues or dreaming happiness out of a drawer of photographs. He forgot her because it was November and the white cotton of his breath unfurled before him, evidence of health and energy.

In the small field Rocky jangled restlessly, making a brittle music. There was the brown magnificence of the horse's flanks glistening, and the flick of muscles now and then like flatfish trapped under the skin. It was his favourite field, a preference that had nothing got to do with shape or with fertility. Just a fine feeling when he stepped in over it. Two chestnut trees hid it from the house so that rounding them and coming towards the gate was contentment and surprise. Never once had a tractor been there. It would have been irreverent, he believed, breaking the brown earth of it by newfangled means.

"Hyup! Hyup!" he cried, searching the sky for rain. They had only begun when the rooks appeared and followed boldly at his heels. Dark, impertinent intruders, they reminded him of his trespasses. Rooks, ravens, crows were birds of mystery, black messengers, bearers of blacker tales. He remembered the Cuchulainn monument, the hurt repose of a warrior, all that drained strength slipping fast under the weird eyes of a raven. He was amplifying all annoyances, discomforting himself. Soon the gulls would be coming inland to scavenge and annoy.

Dempsey hated winter, frosted window panes and the ignominy of water bottles and 'Dick the shepherd blows his nail', an image from an old school reader. All the encumbrances that came and ruined the memory of summer deck-chairs and candy-floss and driving to Tramore to swim in the tide. Meeting a woman perhaps, usually in a dancehall where the

middle-aged invariably seek out their twins because the youngsters' dancing is inimitable and the music available is a strange new dissonance.

Schubert started barking up at the house. Dempsey halted, glanced
down at the buckled steel of the plough and suddenly recalled taking it
from the shed on Monday. There'd been a big rat, dead, behind it when
he lifted. The shameful fear vexed him, fear of a death alone and of dis-
covery later by a stranger, cold and stinking in a place full of snapped
tools and sad bird-cages, their spindled doors hanging open in stiff metal
farewell.

He trotted back up. Schubert sought reward, rolled over on his back
like a glad woman. Dempsey hid his disappointment. It was only Annie
Lydon coming from mass.

"Not a bad day, Annie. I'm down below," and gesturing carelessly
"with the rooks."

"Sure they'd nearly talk to you this weather, Peter. They would. They
would. Well, you won't be robbed so long as Schubert's in charge. I'll say
that."

"Nothing to rob, Annie girl. Sure we're expecting the bailiff any day
now," he joked, displaying the tear in his trousers as a show of poverty.

"Huh! The bailiff, how are you. If I'd the half of what you'll be getting
for the fields, I wouldn't be here talking to you this minute."

They chuckled together as neighbours and old friends. A good soul.
Three children, all reared and 'doing well'. Whatever that was supposed
to imply. Struggling to keep afloat, managing half a foothold on the surface of things. Most of the Goddamn country thinking they were 'doing
well', Dempsey thought. That was the main trouble. Everybody 'doing
well' and no one needing to look beyond himself for succour and peace in
others.

Annie Lydon in her red coat and her chin full of whiskers. At prayer
now, he supposed, the next funeral might be her own. They were lovers
long ago. As before, Dempsey ached at the memory of his hands on her
small breasts in the stables where their clumsy love was played. Hiding
her belongings in various places and then helping her look for them.
These charades of affection. And the long kisses and the warm flimsy
stuff of her frocks. There was happiness then. Music coming from a mar-
quee at the back of the chapel and the Gulliver shadows of those inside
thrown up on the canvas making them afraid as they approached. His girl
who won a basket of wild flowers for having the longest necklace in the
crowd. Real pearl beads or a daisy chain, he couldn't remember.

"Any sign of Dillon on the road?"

"Shouldn't be long now. I passed him below at Sheehan's. It's a queer
business that. Horrid sad," she answered, nodding in that general direc-

tion and departing, her slow comical walk taking her on up over the hill to disappearance the far side of it.

Dempsey agreed curtly and stepped inside and opened a bottle of stout, warm tacky stout from the shelf near the stove where he stocked his adequate supply of booze. She flipped into the kitchen when he drank, haughty and silent still, and she checked the fire again out of habit and not because of any need for another sift of kindling. And he drinking, watched her again, because fixing his eyes nervously on the trees in the window panes or on the angle of books that topped the sideboard, lacking a second bookend, was a trick too bothersome to continue with. Sometimes in the dancehalls he would see a beautiful young girl all frizzed up for the night and looking a little bored with everything and he would start staring at light bulbs or down at the caps of his shoes rather than have the strange one think she was being stared at. But it became too much, this shifting of attention against his real wishes and he would end up staring her restless, till she mooched off to lostness, some spot among the spinning dancers.

Likewise he watched his sister hard now, not trying to conceal it. The way that thin river of inky hair swung about as she stooped, lying flush with her arm one minute, the ribbon perched on her elbow. There was a story in the book by the brothers Grimm about Rapunsel who had long miraculous hair. She was like Rapunsel occasionally, her head full of witches and the rustle of horses going by, the horses of the prince always passing the castles she imagined herself in. Never stopping. Only the frail thunder of the hooves becoming distance.

She deserved a marriage, he thought. More than he did even. It was just ill luck. The way she talked, when she did talk and when she was younger, it seemed impossible she never would. But love for her was the flash and die of a quick spark between two struck stones. She could not have made the effort to sustain it any longer than that. And so she loved the young poacher, handsome in dungarees, she'd seen that evening when she was walking by the estate. He came over the grass with his rifle in one hand and the bunched legs of a pheasant clutched in the other. But he went past, whistling, and the moment was lost forever in her. And back further than that the boy in woollens who gave her the gift of a salmon, a summer's day. She would have married him then if he'd asked, only asked. But it was a gift and no token and so she was left with a dead silver thing in brown paper wrapping and the din of the river sliding past. There had been others too who'd failed to see or take the offers of herself in these brief moments.

He knew these things. She spoke of them as they happened. She wasn't searching for sympathy when she did. It was mere unloading, a cleansing of silliness because the experience had been personal and not shared. Her fingers would pluck absently at her neck and she would tell him everything that happened. Poacher and fisherman and the others. Draining out of her the hurt of them not loving her then. He listened to her and though he knew he'd never want to bring himself to think of things in her way, he could respect her lovingly for being so and not in any way different. If everyone behaved like she did about love it would be like running over stones with eggs in your hands, afraid always of the first stumble. That sort of love was tense and high. He preferred to handle it objectively, steering it himself, grateful for the odd nights of kissing that made the long lack of passion tolerable.

She moved to the window and began picking up objects with no purpose, letting them fall again into their dust rings. She blew into a decanter of pink crystal glass and tugged at the linen dress of a Spanish doll and shook life into the curtains on the window.

He watched her leave the room, again without speaking, chores to be tackled in the rooms upstairs. He rummaged through the leaves of an old newspaper and cut out an advert from an inside page with a nail scissors. 'Sloan's Liniment Relieves Rheumatic Pain'. Intuitively, he rubbed his shoulder where the bitch of a pain was. He flicked the advert over in his hand, revealing a photo of a local wedding, the bride clipped off at the chin, the groom at the shoulders by his rough cutting.

Schubert started off again before he'd time to finish the stout. He eyed the bread knife sunk in a brown loaf and thought how soothing it would be to draw blood, to pierce the neck and watch the nerves jiggling in the hindquarters, the ridiculous after-movement of a leg skipping to and fro. He needed action, a gesture of some sort, fierce and sudden, to ease impatience. A kill would be pleasant. To chuck a hen's neck expertly and feel the feathers slacken in his hands.

The bark persisted, punctuating a human plea. "Whist! Whist up out of that, can't you? That a boy. Itchy-kitchy-kitchy. Good doggie, Schubert."

Dillon's voice.

Dempsey rose and as he moved, tested the small broom of stubble on his face, then cupped his paunch in his hands, the odd shirt buttons straining tightly over it. He'd worried about it at first, stood before mirrors, taking side glances, inhaling. He bought trousers a size too small so that the rind of his belly flopped over the leather belt comically. The deceptions had been hardly worth the effort though. Convincing oneself that one still had an appearance to speak of was sad, like the sadness of a mother going to her daughter's wardrobe and putting on the new dresses and dreaming old occasions, the whole house empty and ripe for foolishness.

"Christ, Peter, he's a fiery devil!" Dillon exclaimed, dropping his bag back into the carrier basket.

"Wouldn't keep him if he wasn't. With the world as it is," he replied blithely, probing a fresh scab that had formed overnight on his cut elbow. Thank God. Sign of health. The healing juices still in working order.

"Well, only the one today. From Dublin. The new stamp's on it too. You'll keep the stamp for me, Peter, like a good man."

"Take it now, sure." Dempsey tore the stamp awkwardly from the envelope. He was trying to fathom why it was he considered it strange that Dillon should be a philatelist. He delivered the mail. Was it that strange so? Maybe it was funny, always doing the obvious.

"You must have a fine store of them now, after all these years," he said, stooping to read.

"Thanks. Oh, thousands. Sure there's no end to them. Only the other day I'd a card from a nephew in Japan with a grand coloured one on it," Dillon said, suddenly conjuring from his contact with films and magazine features, an amateur vision of the orient. Painted girls in costumes and flower gardens and quaint echoing music.

"Any news, Peter?"

"Ah, just an offer for the fields. Not a bad one either. Here, take a look."

Dillon leaned back, blushed and unscrewed the cowls of his handlegrips. The lip service people pay to privacy at the expense of ordinary curiosity. It annoyed Dempsey.

"Go on! Take it, I said. 'Tis nothing that special."

"Fair enough, so. Oh my, he's a fine hand, hasn't he? Holy Christ! That much? Whoever would have thought it?"

Dempsey waited, glad that he'd shown the letter, the intimacy it suggested. Dillon, being postman, was a touchstone for all that happened within a sizable radius of the village. Rightly primed, he'd been known to talk the night long, uncovering secrets, adding flavour to small pieces of rumour. He farted loudly in contentment.

Dillon looked up and, anxious to repay Dempsey's openness some way, decided on a little frivolity. He sniffed like a beagle and pronounced authoritatively, "Stout, I'd say. Bottled stout. Hmmmm . . . gallons of the damn stuff if I've a snout on me at all."

"Wrong!" Dempsey lied, slapping his thigh. "Cabbage. A powerful feed of it last night for supper."

"Is that a fact, now? I'd have sworn it was stout. Well, sure, the one's as lethal as the other, I suppose." Dillon threw his eyes to heaven, fixed them there on a cloud shaped to the likeness of a runner. He pointed up at the grey drift overhead. Dempsey looked, seeing a different image, a rickety circus poodle with its fur blossoming away.

He handed the letter back. "God, Peter, we should all have been bank managers, what? Summer homes and money to burn. Still, I don't know. I can't imagine a bungalow in the fields."

"Well, I can. He can start up a frigging zoo if he likes. As long as the money's good."

They looked to the fields, Dillon trying to recall them, Dempsey well aware of their precise shape and acreage, the quality of pasture, the pepper of thistles that winked in both. He knew the lie of them even before they were his, passing over them with girls who always seemed to have brittle sprigs of lavender pinned to their frocks and he proud of knowing that where they walked would come to him eventually.

"Tell us, Tom. Any bit of news from below in Sheehan's?" Dempsey asked, tracing frail patterns on the ground with his boots.

"Well," the chain of his pocket-watch glistening as he propped out his chest, the local sage with his knuckles folded over his lapels, "from what I can gather, it's a cut-and-dried affair. Time, they say. There's only time in it. Good Lord, 'twould make you weep. Only a youngster. And a pretty little piece too. A sadder business than Jack Cusack's boy, I'd say. Do you remember we took him from the river, Peter? The one side of his face gone. Oh, a desperate sight!"

Dempsey started, holding again the weight of the young boy in his arms, the stamp of unspent money through the wet pockets, and the bruised neck, laying death down under the trees along the riverbank.

"There's no hope for her so, you'd say?"

"I'd say not. Personally like, you know. But, damn it, could a man be one hundred per cent certain the way that mother of hers has played it dead close ever since Timmy died? Your own next-door neighbour and not a word spoken between the pair of you for ages. Sure what kind of carry on is that? Anyway. I'd a parcel for her this morning and the Doctor nearly ran me over when I was coming out the gate. Drove in like the clappers!"

"No!" Dempsey cried incredulously.

"Would I tell a lie? And we were down below in Fitz's the other night, a crowd of us, following that documentary about islands on the box, when in walks Doctor Whelan himself, calling for a rum and coke in that grawnd awcksend of his, you know. So I goes over and asks him has he any bit of news for us. Well, he mutters something about doctor's ethics. Cute-like, wouldn't you know. But I dogs him—what the hell do I care about doctor's ethics—and he finally admits that it's a common complaint that could be deadly. So we came to the conclusion later on, myself and the lads, that it's the man himself. Cancer. Cancer. Now there's a common bastard and right deadly too. Sure what else would have her on the flat of her back these past months and not worth the shifting to a hospital bed. They won't take you in when you're bunched nowadays, Peter."

"True. True." Dempsey plucked a berry from the hedge, pressed it in his fist. "I suppose the village is talking."

"About nothing else. As you'd expect. Gossiping and waiting like vultures. Anyone would think they were above at the Greyhound Derby, one backing cancer and the other undecided. Only the one bit of common ground between them. Beth Sheehan is too fine a girl to be getting the wooden suit so soon," Dillon concluded, hoisting himself up on the saddle and beginning to pedal off. "Good luck, then, Peter. Tell Moira I was asking for her."

"Aye. Good luck, Tom." Dempsey whistled Schubert from off the hall-door mat and headed back down towards the ploughing, stopping a moment on the way when he could catch a view of Sheehan's place beyond the elms. And considering the prospect of the white house, smoking at the centre of a circle of outhouses, thought of the young girl breathing awkwardly under the damp bedclothes within. Her hair gluey with the sweat as if she were drowning in the brown pools of herself, a hurt delicious sinking on past the world of her neat room, its souvenirs and the dreams she hatched in it dissolving in a sweet chaos.

Schubert whined querulously at this delay and Dempsey resumed walking. "Go on! Chase the rooks to hell out of it. Do as you're frigging well told," he cursed.

Rocky whinnied at his return, bubbled about on his hooves, mane shaken out in a floss and the sharp jangle of the buckles. Dempsey halted in wonder sensing the huge power of the awaiting animal like a child plopped under a tumbril and learning the splendour of horses for the first time. The neck, legs, and balls, the supple rhythms of its shuffling there although draped in the gear of ploughing. There were the heavy imprints of restlessness on the earth, the crescent-web of bored hooves. They breathed out the white air of November, Rocky's pink nostrils flickering and the mouth daubed with froth. The alchemy of making the air visible linked them both together, beast and ploughman, so that it sickened him to have to clasp again the burnished wood of the handles and march behind the crazy tail, the lithe bunching of horse muscle.

And as they worked the field up and down Dempsey felt the old delight in bringing up furrows fading like the frail dappled wings of some exotic bird flying to darkness in his mind. The thud of footwork and the rare gathering dance of the horse's flanks seemed to be telling him something, an endless echo of insinuation about himself that could not be shut away.

The nausea soon became worn down to a faint unease with the business of ploughing. Schubert kept the rooks from his heels. But then they careered overhead, bringing the dog to its hind legs. Dempsey decided to clean out the gun that evening. Tomorrow would tell a different tale. They'd burst like clay pigeons over the cut earth. "Come on! Come on! Pester me to hell out of it!" he roared, giddily anticipating the sport with bullets, the black birds exploding in mid-air, plummeting down dead like torn kites.

When Schubert came barking over and snapping at his trousers, Dempsey kicked out at the dog, annoyed. He clipped him on the backside but still there was no stopping him. When he looked around he saw her approach through the near field, bandy legs wobbling over grass and her blue scarf clicking. Mrs. Sheehan rested one arm on the open gate and picked absently at her teeth. Dempsey sighed, buttoned his waistcoat and trotted eagerly towards her.

Schubert felt the cool fan of Rocky's breath on him and he flounced down under it, coat-twitching, red sopping tongue darting out over his paws. And though the gestures of Dempsey and the woman made no sense to him, his eyes stayed riveted on the pair of them. He saw her, squat and determined-looking, and her skirts go rippling whenever she shifted from one foot to the other. And Dempsey, all arms and fingers and questions, working a hand through his hair back to the nape of the neck where it fidgeted with his shirt-collar. A letter was exchanged and she reading a little of it, then putting it down and talking before taking it up again to read some more. And then Dempsey taking the letter back and ramming it into his waistcoat pocket.

And, "Stay, Schubert! Stay! That's a good boy," he said as he walked out of the field, Mrs. Sheehan pecking her way after him in her loose sombre clothes like a weird mechanised scarecrow.

They both diminished to the size of blurred pencils as they grew further and further away and by the time they'd got to Sheehan's place they'd become invisible and the birds streamed down where they'd walked, cackling raggedly.

When Dempsey got back home to the house she was in the kitchen peeling apples, slicing the white shreds into a saucepan at her feet on the floor, tossing the crits and the rinds into a basin. He saw that she'd let out her hair and that it swarmed loosely around her, running over her wrists and coming up off them when she raised her head to study him quickly. She'd the purple jumper with the v-neck on her and her fine beige shirt. And tasting again that scent of milk and wet timber that she sometimes carried with her into rooms, he was more sorry than ever for her lack of love, a man, if needs be, who would come towards her in the evening, walking confidently, the shot pheasant dangling in his fist and who'd stop and love her and not go by, whistling, leaving her disappointed in her warm clothes.

But that idea of love was strange and seldom. Maybe she ought to have been told or seen from life itself that people met by accident and coupled and parted in the morning with their hair tossed, forgetting the dark room and the swinging flex of the light bulb when they became anonymous and separate again, doing their day's business. Love was foreign to the dream of a young boy with salmon on a riverbank. It was often the disarray of a man thinking and a woman crying on pillows.

If she never came round to an acceptance of that, she would have to go on guarding her brittle egg of love, picking her meticulous routes over stones that would never end under her crazy feet.

Dempsey knew she'd continue as before, always. He came up close to her and went down on his hunkers beside her chair. He ducked his hand into the saucepan of apples and diced a small piece slowly palm to palm.

"A girl, Moira," he said. "A girl . . . I wanted that."

She stopped peeling and flicked her hair back softly over her shoulders. "A girl!" she whispered, smiling into the basin of rinds.

Staying close there over the tang of apples, they felt the silence of the kitchen break when they heard Schubert bark from somewhere far down in the fields. It was his duty to.

The Contributors

JOHN BANVILLE was born in County Wexford in 1946. He has published four books: *Long Lankin* (1970), *Nightspawn* (1971), *Birchwood* (1973), and *Doctor Copernicus* (1976), all published by Secker and Warburg. He is a journalist and lives in Dublin.

SAMUEL BECKETT is Ireland's greatest living author. He was born in Dublin in 1906 and studied at Trinity College, Dublin, where he later taught briefly. He travelled, studied and taught in Europe before settling in Paris in the 1930s where he was closely associated with James Joyce. He was honoured by the French government for his active work in the Resistance. He writes in English and French and has published poems, prose (including *Murphy, Watt, Molloy, Malone Dies, The Unnameable, The Lost Ones* and *How It Is*) and plays (including *Waiting for Godot, Endgame, Krapp's Last Tape* and *Happy Days*). In 1969 he won the Nobel Prize. He continues to write fiction and drama and is actively involved in staging new productions of his plays. He lives in Paris.

EAVAN BOLAND was born in Dublin in 1945. In 1968 she was awarded the Macauley Fellowship for poetry. She has published two books: *New Territory* (1967), Allen Figgis Ltd., and *The War Horse* (1975), Gollancz. She lives and teaches in Dublin.

EDWARD BRAZIL was born in Dublin in 1954 and studied at Trinity College, Dublin. His first story was published in 1974 and the following year he won a Hennessy Literary Award. He now teaches in Dublin.

CIARAN CARSON was born in Belfast in 1948 and his first language was Irish. He studied at Queen's University, Belfast, and is now Traditional Arts Officer with the Arts Council of Northern Ireland. In

1976 he published *The New Estate* (Blackstaff/Wake Forest University Press). He lives in Belfast.

EILÉAN NÍ CHUILLEANÁIN was born in Cork city in 1942 and educated at University College, Cork, and Oxford. In 1973 she won the Patrick Kavanagh Award for her first collection, *Acts and Monuments* (1972), Gallery Press. Her other books are *Site of Ambush* (1975), *Cork*, with drawings by Brian Lalor (1977), Gallery Press, and *The Second Voyage: A Selection* (1977), Gallery/Wake Forest University Press. She teaches at Trinity College, Dublin.

HARRY CLIFTON was born in Dublin in 1952 and studied at University College. Two collections, *The Walls of Carthage* (1977) and *Office of the Salt Merchant* (1979), were published by the Gallery Press. He now lives in Dublin.

SEAMUS DEANE was born in Derry in 1940. He studied at Queen's University, Belfast, and at Cambridge. He has taught in several American universities and has published two collections of poems: *Gradual Wars* (1972), Irish University Press, and *Rumours* (1977), Dolmen Press. He teaches at University College and lives in Dublin.

EILÍS DILLON was born in Galway in 1920. She has written many books for children including *The Lost Island* (1952), *The San Sebastian* (1953), *The House on the Shore* (1955) and *The Island of the Horses* (1956), all from Faber and Faber. Her recent novels, *Across the Bitter Sea* (1973) and *Blood Relations* (1978), were published by Hodder and Stoughton/Simon and Schuster. She translated *The Voyage of Mael Duin* (1969), Faber, and has lived in Rome and America. Her home is in Dublin.

PAUL DURCAN was born in Dublin in 1944 and studied at University College, Cork. In 1974 he won the Patrick Kavanagh Award and published his first collection, *O Westport in the Light of Asia Minor* (Anna Livia, Dublin). In 1976 he was awarded an Arts Council Bursary and published *Teresa's Bar* (Gallery Press). In 1978, he published *Sam's Cross* (Profile Poetry). He lives in Cork.

JOHN ENNIS was born in Westmeath in 1944. He now lives in Waterford where he teaches at the Regional College and the Central Technical Institute. In 1975 he won the Patrick Kavanagh Award for poetry and he has published three collections, *Night on Hibernia* (1976), *Dolmen Hill* (1977), *A Drink of Spring* (1979), all from Gallery Press.

MICHAEL HARTNETT was born in County Limerick in 1941. The Dolmen
Press published his first collection, *Anatomy of a Cliché*, in 1968.
He has since published *Selected Poems* (1970), New Writers' Press,
and a version of the *Tao*, as well as translations of Old Irish and
works of Garcia Lorca. *A Farewell to English* (1975; enl. edn.
1978), Gallery Press, followed his declaration that he would write
only in Irish from then on. *Poems in English* (Dolmen) appeared in
1977 and *Adharca Broic*, his first collection in Irish, was published
by Gallery Press in 1978. He lives in County Limerick.

DERMOT HEALY was born in Westmeath in 1947. He has published poems
and stories and has won two Hennessy Literary Awards. In 1977 he
was granted an Irish Arts Council Bursary for creative writing. He
now lives in County Cavan.

SEAMUS HEANEY was born on a farm in County Derry in 1939. He attended
Queen's University, Belfast, where he later taught. He has published five collections of poems: *Death of a Naturalist* (1966), *Door
into the Dark* (1969), *Wintering Out* (1972), *North* (1975) and *Field
Work* (1979), all from Faber and Faber. He now lives in Dublin
where he heads the English Department at Carysfort College of
Education.

JOHN HEWITT was born in Belfast in 1907 and studied at Queen's University. His *Collected Poems 1932-67* was published in 1968 by Mac-
Gibbon and Kee, and he has since published *Out of My Time*
(1974), *Time Enough* (1976), and *The Rain Dance* (1978), all from
Blackstaff. He lives in Belfast and has recently published books on
art and artists.

AIDAN HIGGINS was born in County Kildare in 1927. He has lived exten-
sively in Africa, Spain and England and has published a book of
stories, *Felo de Se* (1960), *Images of Africa: Diary 1956-60* (1971)
and the novels *Langrishe, Go Down* (1966), *Balcony of Europe*
(1972), all from John Calder; and *Scenes from a Receding Past*
(1977), his most recent novel, has been published by John Calder/
Riverrun. He edited *A Century of Short Stories* (1977), Cape. His
home is in London.

PEARSE HUTCHINSON was born in Glasgow, of Irish parents, in 1927, and
reared in Dublin from 1932. He has published four collections of
poems in English: *Tongue without Hands* (1963) and *Expansions*

(1969), both from Dolmen Press; *Watching the Morning Grow* (1972) and *The Frost Is All Over* (1975), both Gallery Press; as well as a book of poems in Irish, *Faoistin Bhacach* (1968), An Clóchomhar; and translations from Catalan, *Joseph Garner: 30 Poems* (1962), Dolphin Books, Oxford; and from Galaicoportuguese, *Friends Songs: Medieval Love-Poems* (1970), New Writers' Press, Dublin. *Selected Poems* is forthcoming from Gallery Press. He lives in Dublin.

JOHN JORDAN was born in Dublin in 1930 and studied at University College where he later taught. He has published three collections of prose and poetry: *A Raft from Flotsam* (1975), *Blood and Stations* (1976), both from Gallery Press; and *Yarns* (1977), Poolbeg Press. He is a journalist, a broadcaster and a Dubliner.

NEIL JORDAN was born in Sligo in 1951 and studied at University College, Dublin. He is a founder-member of The Irish Writers' Co-operative which published *Night in Tunisia*, a collection of stories, in 1976. In the same year the Irish Arts Council awarded him a Bursary for literature. He lives in Dublin.

BRENDAN KENNELLY was born in County Kerry in 1936 and studied at Trinity College, Dublin, where he now teaches, and at Leeds. He has published two novels and edited the *Penguin Book of Irish Verse*. His collections of poetry include *Dream of a Black Fox* (1968), Allen Figgis, *Selected Poems* (1969), Figgis/Dutton, and *New and Selected Poems* (1976) and *A Small Light*, both from Gallery Press. He lives in Dublin.

THOMAS KILROY was born in 1934. He has written four plays: *The Death and Resurrection of Mr. Roche* (1969), Faber and Faber, *The O'Neill, Tea and Sex and Shakespeare*, and *Talbot's Box* (1979), Gallery Press; a novel, *The Big Chapel* (1971), Faber, and plays for radio and television. He teaches at University College, Galway.

THOMAS KINSELLA was born in Dublin in 1927 and studied at University College. He left a career in the Department of Finance to teach in America. He has published *Another September* (1958), *Downstream* (1962), *Nightwalker and Other Poems* (1968), *Selected Poems, 1956–68* (1973), *New Poems 1973, Fifteen Dead*, and *One and Other Poems* (1979), all from Dolmen Press; several titles from his own Peppercanister imprint; and *Poems 1956–73* and *One:*

Poems 1973–78, both 1979 Wake Forest University Press. He translated *The Táin,* a translation of the Irish epic *Táin Bó Cuailnge,* in 1969. He now divides his time between Temple University in Philadelphia and Dublin.

MARY LAVIN was born in Massachusetts in 1912, grew up in Ireland and studied at University College, Dublin. Her books include *The Stories of Mary Lavin,* Volume One (1964), Volume Two (1974), and *A Memory and Other Stories* (1977), all by Constable, London, and *Tales from Bective Bridge* (1978), Poolbeg. Houghton-Mifflin published her *Collected Stories* in 1971 and *The Shrine and Other Stories* in 1977 in America. She has taught in America and now divides her time between Dublin and County Meath.

MICHAEL LONGLEY was born in Belfast in 1939 and educated at Trinity College, Dublin. He has published three collections of poems: *No Continuing City* (1969), Macmillan, *An Exploded View* (1973), and *Man Lying on a Wall* (1976), both from Gollancz. *The Echo Gate* is to be published in 1979. He is now Assistant Director of the Arts Council of Northern Ireland. He lives in Belfast.

EUGENE MCCABE was born in County Monaghan in 1930. His plays include *King of the Castle* (1978), Gallery Press/Proscenium, *Swift, Daybreak,* and *Pull Down a Horseman,* and he has published *Victims: a Tale from Fermanagh* (1976) and *Heritage* (1978), both from Gollancz. Much of his work has been televised. He lives in County Monaghan.

JOHN MCGAHERN was born in Dublin in 1935 and grew up in various parts of the West of Ireland. He has published three novels: *The Barracks* (1963), *The Dark* (1965) and *The Leavetaking* (1974), and two collections of short stories: *Nightlines* (1970) and *Getting Through* (1978), all from Faber and Faber. He has taught in Ireland, England and America, and lives in County Leitrim.

DEREK MAHON was born in Belfast in 1941 and studied at Trinity College, Dublin. He has published three collections of poems: *Night-Crossing* (1968), *Lives* (1972) and *The Snow Party* (1975), all from Oxford University Press. He edited the *Sphere Book of Modern Irish Poetry* in 1972. He lived in England for several years before returning to Ireland in 1977 to become the first Writer-in-Residence at the New University of Ulster at Coleraine. *Poems 1962–1978* is forthcoming from Oxford University Press.

JOHN MONTAGUE was born of Irish parents in Brooklyn in 1929 and grew up in County Tyrone. He lived and taught in Paris for many years. He has published *Death of a Chieftain and Other Stories* (1964) and six collections of poems: *Poisoned Lands* (1961, revised edition 1977), Dolmen/Oxford; *A Chosen Light* (1967), MacGibbon and Kee; *Tides* (1970), Dolmen/Swallow; *The Rough Field* (1972), Dolmen/Oxford; *A Slow Dance* (1975), and *The Great Cloak* (1978), both Dolmen/Oxford/Wake Forest University Press). He edited *The Faber Book of Irish Verse* (1974; American edition, 1977, Macmillan, N.Y.). He lives in Cork where he teaches at University College.

PAUL MULDOON was born in County Armagh in 1951 and studied at Queen's University, Belfast. He has published two books of poetry: *New Weather* (1973), Faber and Faber, and *Mules* (1977), Faber/Wake Forest University Press. He lives in Belfast and is a radio producer for the BBC (N. Ireland).

RICHARD MURPHY was born in County Galway in 1927 and spent part of his childhood in Ceylon. He studied at Oxford and at the Sorbonne. His books are *Sailing to an Island* (1963), *The Battle of Aughrim* (1968), *High Island* (1974) and *Selected Poems* (1979), all Faber and Faber; and *High Island: New and Selected Poems* (1974), Harper and Row. He travels widely and has taught at several English and American universities. His home is in Cleggan, County Galway.

THOMAS MURPHY was born in County Galway in 1935. He retired from teaching in 1962 to become a full-time writer and lived in England for several years. He has written many plays including *On the Outside/On the Inside* (1976), Gallery Press; *A Crucial Week in the Life of a Grocer's Assistant* (1978), Gallery/Proscenium Press; *The Morning After Optimism* (1973), Mercier Press; and *The Sanctuary Lamp* (1976), Poolbeg Press. He is a director of the Abbey Theatre and lives in Dublin.

LIAM O'FLAHERTY was born on the Aran Islands in 1896 and studied at University College, Dublin. He fought in World War I and returned to Ireland in time to fight in the Irish Revolution and the Civil War. Afterwards he left Ireland, disappointed with the outcome, and spent some time in America. His first novel was published in 1923. He is a master of the Irish short story form and his books include

The Informer (1925), *The Puritan* (1932), *Famine* (1937), *Land* (1946), *Pedlar's Revenge and Other Stories* (1976), *Skerrett* (1977), *The Wilderness* (1978), and *The Ecstacy of Angus* (1978), all from Wolfhound Press. He lives in Dublin.

DESMOND O'GRADY was born in Limerick in 1935 and studied at Harvard under John V. Kelleher. He has lived and taught in Paris, Cairo and Rome and was closely associated with Ezra Pound. He has published eight books of poems including *The Dark Edge of Europe* (1967), *The Dying Gaul* (1968), both from MacGibbon and Kee; *Separations* (1973), The Goldsmith Press; *Sing Me Creation* (1977), and *The Headgear of the Tribe: New and Selected Poems* (1978), both from the Gallery Press; and translations in *Off Licence* (1968), *The Gododdin* (1977), both from Dolmen; and *A Limerick Rake* (1978), Gallery Press. He lives on a Greek island.

FRANK ORMSBY was born in 1947 in County Fermanagh and studied at Queen's University, Belfast. He now teaches in Belfast and edits *The Honest Ulsterman*. *A Store of Candles* (Oxford University Press), a Poetry Society Choice, was published in 1977. He lives in Belfast.

JAMES SIMMONS was born in Derry in 1933 and studied at Leeds. He founded *The Honest Ulsterman* in 1968. He has published seven books of poetry including *West Strand Visions* (1974), *Judy Garland and the Cold War* (1976), and *The Selected James Simmons* (1978), all by Blackstaff Press; and recorded many of his own songs. He edited *Ten Irish Poets* (1974), Carcanet. He teaches at the New University of Ulster (Coleraine) and lives in Portrush.

FRANCIS STUART was born in Australia of Irish parents in 1902. His first book was a collection of poems and he has since published many novels including *Memorial* (1973), Southern Illinois University Press/Martin, Brian and O'Keefe; *The Pillar of Cloud* (1948, 1974), *Redemption* (1950, 1974), both Martin, Brian, and O'Keefe; *Black List, Section H* (1971, 1975), Southern Illinois University Press/Martin, Brian, and O'Keefe; and *A Hole in the Head* (1977), Longship Press. He lived in Germany during World War II. He now lives in Dublin.

The Editors

PETER FALLON was born 26 February 1951 and grew up on a farm in County Meath. In 1970 he founded the Gallery Press and has since then edited and published Ireland's foremost poetry series. An Honours graduate of Trinity College, Dublin, he has been poet-in-residence at Deerfield Academy in Massachusetts and he regularly tours America giving lectures and readings of his work. *The Speaking Stones* (1978), Gallery Press, is his fourth book of poems. He lives in Loughcrew in County Meath.

SEÁN GOLDEN was born 26 February 1948 in London, of Irish parents. He spent part of his childhood in the west of Ireland before his family emigrated to America. He received his Ph.D. from the University of Connecticut where he has also taught. He now teaches at the University of Notre Dame and divides his time between Ireland and America. He lectures frequently at international conferences on Joyce, Celtic Art, Irish literature and music, and American poetry, and has published work on these subjects. His home is near Ballaghaderreen.